I CAN DO THAT!
FURNITURE PROJECTS

20 Easy & Fun Woodworking Projects to Build Your Skills

Chad Stanton

POPULAR WOODWORKING BOOKS

CINCINNATI, OHIO

WWW.POPULARWOODWORKING.COM

DEDICATION

This book is dedicated to my father-in-law HanSang Kim who treats me like his real son, to my mother Linda Stanton who passed away during its writing and in appreciation of the love and support of my wife BoHyun Kim and good friend, "Safety" Dan Kine.

ACKNOWLEDGMENTS

Special thanks to David Thiel, Ric Deliantoni and Scott Francis for their understanding and cooperation, and for working with me during a very difficult time in my life.

Table of Contents

Curved Legged Coffee Table

The living room is a great place for friends or family to gather for any social occasion. It's a place to relax, unwind and have a drink or two. Of course, you'll need someplace to set that drink. This coffee table has plenty of space for setting things on top, and it also has a drawer on the front to store coasters, remote controls or anything else you wish to keep out of sight. It's not only functional, it's quite attractive. The curved legs and the two-tone stain give this table a graceful look, making it a perfect centerpiece for the living room.

Since this is a larger project, construction from solid wood can be costly, so I've designed it so you can make most of it from a single sheet of plywood. Perfect for limiting the strain on the wallet. But it's not all plywood – the curved legs are solid wood.

Begin this coffee table by making the plywood top. From the cut list, measure over from the edge of the plywood and make a pencil line. Use a straight-line jig for the circular saw and make a cut going with grain. The jig has a fence to guide the saw, and because the fence is perfectly in line with the blade it can be placed right on the line for an accurate cut **(Photo 1)**.

Use sacrificial boards underneath the plywood. Make sure to have the boards running perpendicular to the cut. This practice keeps the plywood from falling in on itself and pinching or binding the blade when making the cut.

When using the circular saw, place the good side of the plywood face-down. Crosscutting plywood produces some tear-out on the top surface, leaving a very rough and jagged edge. To help eliminate this make a shallow cut first into the plywood. This is called a scoring cut.

Set the blade so it cuts no more than ⅛" into the plywood and make the scoring cut **(Photo 2)**.

Then, without moving the jig, adjust the blade depth to make the full cut.

With the top cut to size, repeat the same procedure for cutting out the lower shelf.

Although the veneer faces of the plywood tabletop and lower shelf look fine, the rough plywood edges stick out like a sore thumb. Use edge banding to cover up the layers of plywood. Edge banding is a thin strip of veneer available in various wood species – in this case I've chosen banding in oak to match the oak plywood – and has a heat-activated adhesive on the back, which can be applied using a common household iron.

When applying edge banding, common sense would say to cut the banding the same length as the edge being covered. However, as the glue begins to melt the edge band has a the tendency to slide. If the banding is the exact length, it might move from the original position and expose the plywood layers that I wanted to cover up. To avoid this,

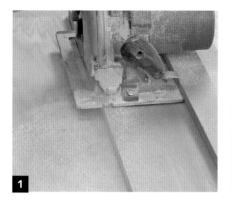

leave banding a little long and cut off the ends with a razor or knife after the glue sets.

The glue sets fairly quickly once the heat is removed. Still, it's not a bad idea, while the edge banding is still warm, to use a scrap piece of wood to rub back and forth on the banding with some pressure to help make sure the banding is firmly applied.

Use a razor blade to cut off the long ends. Edge banding is typically a bit wider than the plywood, so you'll need to trim this flush, too. There is a tool that fits over the plywood and it is squeezed together tightly around both sides of the banding. It has two blades in it and while squeezing, push the tool to cut the excess waste off the banding. However, some tear out can occur while using this tool. Edge banding is real wood, and just like real wood going against the grain can produce tear-out. So while one side of the tool is cutting with the grain, the other side is going against the grain. *TIP – Separate the tool into two halves and trim each side individually, making sure to go with the grain* **(Photo 3)**.

Once the top is done, set it aside and begin work on the table aprons. The aprons are plywood trimmed down to 2¹/₂" with a circular saw guided by a straightedge or auxiliary fence. Crosscut the aprons to length on the miter saw. Lay the apron pieces out according to the plans and mark where the pocket holes will go. Pocket screws will attach the aprons together as well as fasten the top **(Photo 4)**.

Glue and screw the apron assembly together and set the assembly aside.

The legs are made from 1x8 solid oak, and each has a slight curve. Make a template from the plans, then use a pencil to trace the pattern onto each of the leg workpieces.

Notice that the template goes from one corner to the other of the 1x8 **(Photo 5)**.

Cut out the legs with a jigsaw and clean up any rough edges with a file or sandpaper.

It's time for some assembly. From the plans, measure up and mark where the lower shelf will be positioned and use pocket screws to attach the legs to the shelf **(Photo 6)**.

After all four legs are attached to the shelf, turn the table upside down and place the apron assembly inside of the legs. This keeps the top of the legs flush with the top of the apron assembly. Measure an equal distance from side to side to get the apron assembly centered in the legs. Clamp the aprons to the legs to hold it in place, then drill clearance holes through the back side of the aprons. Finally, screw the apron assembly to the back side of the legs.

It might be tempting to attach the top, but the drawer is next. And with the top off, it will be easier to get the measurements needed for the drawer.

Measurements for the drawer size can be found in the plans, however it's best to measure the inside of the drawer opening in the apron to get an exact measurement. Keep in mind, this drawer uses glides, which will make opening it easier. The two most common types of glides are the ³/₄" extension (right) and the full extension (left) *TIP – most drawer glides require ¹/₂" clearance, so a good rule of thumb is to make the drawer 1" smaller than the opening* **(Photo 7)**.

The drawer is made out of ¹/₂" x 3¹/₂" poplar cut down to the correct height. The drawer construction is simple on these, with the sides glued and nailed using butt joints. The bottom is ¹/₄" plywood cut to the size of the drawer frame

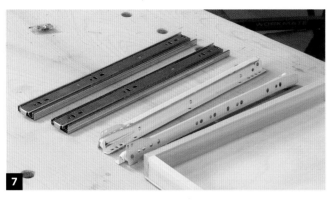

and, again, glued and nailed to the bottom of the drawer frame **(Photo 8)**.

Using the ³/₄" extension glides, mount one part of the glide to the drawer bottom and keep it flush with the front of the drawer. On the table, mount the second half of the glide ³/₄" back from the front edge – this will account for the thickness of the drawer front.

With the drawer mounted in the table, the drawer front is next. The drawer front is some of the ³/₄" plywood cut slightly smaller than the apron opening. Making the drawer front a bit smaller than the opening ensures that it won't rub on the underside of the tabletop or sides of the apron opening once installed. Likewise, shaving just a bit off the drawer front dimensions allows you to add edge banding around the edges to hide the raw plywood if you like. Keep the drawer front flush with the bottom edge of the apron **(Photo 9)**.

Use spring clamps to hold the drawer front in place. From inside the drawer, drill clearance holes through the front and into the back surface of the drawer front, then secure the drawer front with screws **(Photo 10)**.

Test that the drawer opens and closes smoothly.

Place the tabletop top-side down on your bench, then flip the table upside down on the underside of the tabletop. Center the table on the top and place pocket screws in one back corner. Check the front of drawer. It should be flush to the apron with even gaps. If not, slightly pull or push the front legs until alignment is corrected. Then finish driving screws all around the apron.

Return the table to its upright position, then sand and finish as desired. However, the veneer is very thin so be careful not to sand too deeply into the plywood. (*A link to the ICDT common rules manual is located at the end of the book*).

I did this project with a two-toned stain color – natural for the top, lower shelf, apron and drawer, and a dark walnut for the legs. If you choose to do this, carefully mask off where the two colors will intersect to prevent bleeding into other area.

This table has three coats of oil-based polyurethane finish to offer better protection from hot and cold items placed on the surface.

Your finished table will be perfect for holding coffee cups, TV remotes or books – I'd also be willing to bet it will hold the interest of all who see it.

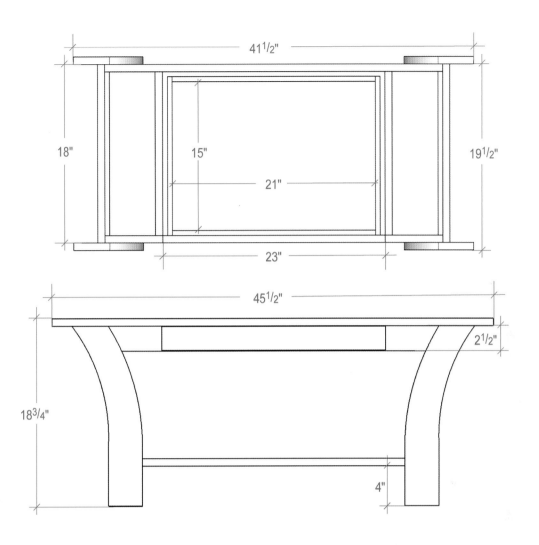

Parts list in inches

QTY.	PART	THICKNESS	WIDTH	LENGTH
1	top	$3/4$	$21^1/_2$	$45^1/_2$
1	shelf	$3/4$	18	34
4	legs	$3/4$	$7^1/_4$	18
1	back apron	$3/4$	$2^1/_2$	35
2	inside aprons	$3/4$	$2^1/_2$	$16^1/_2$
2	outside aprons	$3/4$	$2^1/_2$	18
2	front aprons	$3/4$	$2^1/_2$	6
1	drawer front	$3/4$	$2^1/_2$	23
2	drawer sides	$1/2$	$1^3/_8$	16
2	drawer F & B	$1/2$	$1^3/_8$	21
1	drawer bottom	$1/4$	16	22

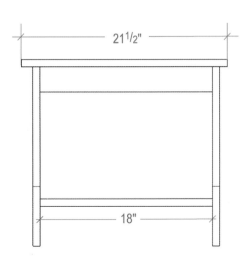

Puzzle Leg Coffee Table

As a kid, I remember wooden puzzles that always seemed to have some kind of trick that defied the laws of nature. Just for fun I decided to make one that gives the impression that the three pieces of wood have pierced through each other. Then I thought to myself, "Hey, that could make a cool coffee table." And so with a few 2x6s and some plywood the process of building one began.

This project isn't overly complicated, but it does require accurate measuring and cutting. Each of the three pieces is the same length and width. The width of the pieces has to be three times the thickness of each piece. There are notches cut into them (**Photo 1 sample**), and then the secret of the assembly order is key to putting it all together.

The top of this coffee table is comprised of two pieces of 3/4" plywood glued and screwed together. I really liked the look of the plywood grain but it was a little busy. Routing a few grooves in the surface softened the effect of the grain and gives the impression of several boards planked together.

The legs are cut to length from 2x6 dimensional lumber. Crosscut the legs to 36" in length on the miter saw. As noted, the width of each leg is three times its thickness. A standard 2x6 is actually 1½"-thick so the width of each board is 4½". You'll have to rip the boards down to get that width. Also 2x6s have slightly rounded over corners that have to be squared before they'll fit into the notches without gaps.

If you have access to a table saw, squaring those edges and ripping the boards to the proper width is easy. However, you can still accomplish this with a circular saw and an auxiliary saw guide attached to rip it to width. Cut equal amounts off each edge to get the 4½" width (**Photo 2**), and that will automatically square the edges as well. These cuts have to be precise, so rip the board just a little wider, then use a handplane to sneak up on the exact size.

Now, let's get those boards ready for some notching. Lay the three legs out so the ends are flush with each other. Find the middle of the boards and draw a line across them (**Photo 3**). Then measure 2¼" over on both sides of that line, making new lines (**Photo 4**). This is the width of the board.

Transfer these three lines all the way around to the other side of each board.

Use a combination square and set it to the thickness of the board. Run the combination square down each side of the board and draw a line. This will define the width of the notch you'll cut (**Photo 5**).

Two of the three legs will be notched almost the exact same way. However the third one is different so set it aside and begin with the first two (**Photo 6**).

Use a Forstner bit to remove the majority of the waste to form your notch. Find the center of the board so the point of the bit can be placed on the line (**Photo 7**).

Drill the two ends of the notch first and then the middle. When using a drill it's easy to bore a hole off at a slight angle. To help prevent this, drill about halfway and then flip the board over to repeat the process. This helps assure straight, square holes. (Make sure you have a sacrificial board underneath to protect the benchtop).

With the holes drilled, square up the notch with a 3/4" chisel. Begin working the chisel with the grain of the board. Slowly work to the pencil line, but don't go beyond it. Also, just like when drilling, chisel about half way and then turn the board over (**Photo 8**).

TIP – Working the chisel at a slight angle produces a slicing effect versus a chopping effect, making it easier to work.

To square up the corners, strike the chisel with a mallet,

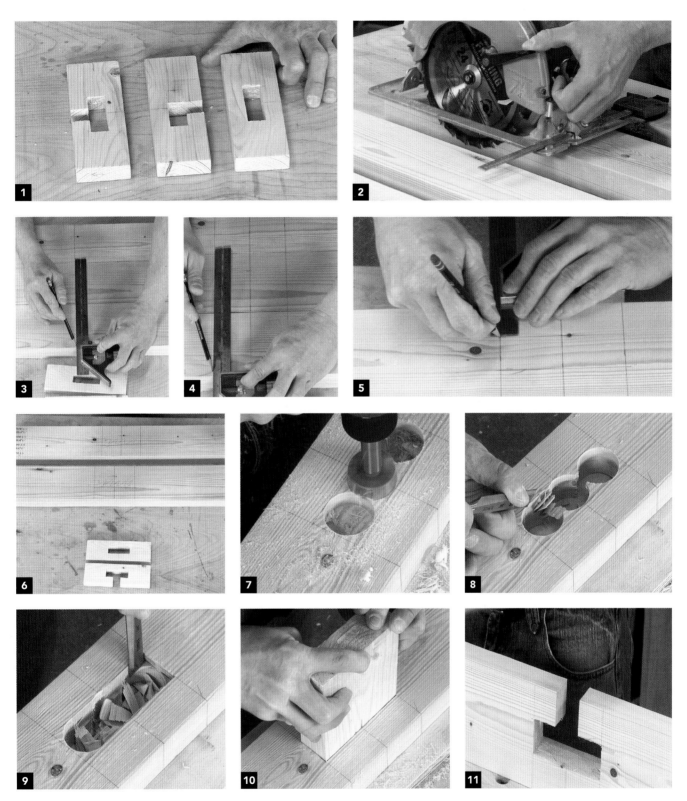

going across the grain, then strike the chisel going with the grain **(Photo 9)**. Remove a little at time until reaching the middle and again flip the board over for the other side. *TIP – When striking a chisel with a mallet, place the workpiece on the bench directly over the leg of the bench. This is the sturdiest part of the bench and will reduce any bounce giving a better, deep cut.*

After using the chisel, test-fit the notch with a scrap piece of the leg **(Photo 10)**. It should be snug with no gaps. If the notch is too small, use a rasp and adjust the fit to where the piece goes in but is not loose. If the fit is really tight, do not strike with a mallet to get the piece to fit. This could result in splitting the leg.

After a nice fit is achieved on the first leg, drill and mortise the notch out the same way for the second leg. Although the notch in this leg is the same as in the first, this one gets a secondary notch perpendicular to it. The crosscut

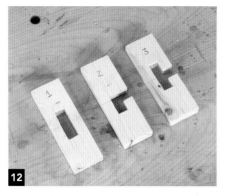

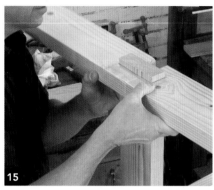

section to be removed matches the thickness of the leg at 1 1/2". Measure and draw the line and cut it out with a hand saw (**Photo 11**). Make sure to cut on the waste side of the line. Once again, if the test piece is too tight, trim the notch with a rasp or sanding block.

The third and last leg is drilled and cut out in the same manner as the other two, but pay attention to the size and shape of the material being removed. From the plans, lay out the lines and remove the waste.

With all three legs notched out, it's time for a test fit. Just like my original small puzzle pieces (**Photo 12**), fitting the legs together requires that it be done in a specific order. It helps to number the pieces to keep from getting confused.

Place leg number 1 vertical in the vise and slide number 2 into it (**Photo 13**).

Slide number 2 to the edge of the notch keeping it flush with the face on leg number 1. Make sure the notch on leg 2 is facing toward you and not away from you (**Photo 14**).

Leg number 3 slides down from the top of leg number 1. Again note the direction of the notch cut out. It's facing away from me (**Photo 15**).

Leg 3 has to fit over and into leg number 2. This will be a snug fit, but do not strike it with a mallet or it will break (**Photo 16**).

Once number 3 is in place, finish the fit by pushing leg number 2 deeper into number 1 (**Photo 17**). Now the test-fit is a success!

With the legs setting on top of the workbench, cut the bottoms so they sit flat. Use a compass and set it to the highest corner of the leg (**Photo 18**).

Then trace a pencil line all the way around the leg. Do this for each leg, then turn the unit over, and again trace

around each leg. The tops are also cut flat for the top to be attached.

Disassemble the leg unit to cut each of the individual legs. You can use a miter saw for this cut, however it has to be a compound miter saw that not only pivots in the front, but has to be able to tilt both directions in the back. If a compound miter saw isn't available, do the crosscutting by hand with a handsaw (**Photo 19**).

When using the handsaw, begin by sawing down the line a little in the back, then tilt the saw forward to cut the line on the top. Repeat this procedure. Work slowly and pay attention to the lines. Once the blade is about one third into the wood it won't be possible to correct the angle of the saw (**Photo 20**).

Reassemble the leg unit and then drill some clearance holes on the tops of the legs. This will allow you to drive screws up and through the legs to attach the top (**Photo 21**).

The table top is a double layer of 3/4" plywood cut into 3' squares, with line drawn on the upper piece at 6" spacing. We'll rout along these lines to give the top a simulated planking effect (**Photo 22**). To make these V-shaped grooves we'll use what's called a "veining bit" with a triangular tip (**Photo 23**).

Go ahead and chuck the bit up in your router so that just the triangular tip extends past the router's base plate.

To make sure our router cuts are straight, clamp a straightedge onto the plywood to guide the router. To accurately locate the straightedge, take a compass and adjust it so the points extend from the edge of the router base to the center of the router bit (**Photo 24**).

Now, place the compass point on the line and make a mark with the pencil end. Do this at both ends of all the

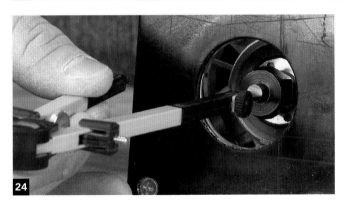

lines. Next, clamp a straightedge on the outside of the compass marks **(Photo 25)**.

Keep the router firmly against the straightedge, then move it smoothly across the plywood to create the first groove. Unclamp and move the straightedge to the next line and so on to complete the top **(Photo 26)**.

Now let's glue up the top and cut it to shape. Draw a circle on the bottom side of the second piece of plywood. *TIP – Just like regular wood, plywood can bow. If that is the case, have the two bowed pieces opposing each other. This way when they are screwed together the outside edges will be nice and tight with no gaps.*

To do this, first find the center of the plywood by drawing lines from the corners – where they cross is the center. Drive a nail into one end of a piece of scrap and drill a pencil hole 18" from the nail. (This little contraption is called a "trammel," by the way.) Tap the nail into the plywood, stick a pencil into the other hole at the other and rotate the scrap to draw your circle **(Photo 27)**.

Spread glue on the inside of both pieces and stack them together, making sure that your circle is oriented out at the bottom and your routed grooves out at the top.

Clamp the two pieces together. Drill equally spaced clearance holes around the circumference of the bottom piece, being careful not to not drill all the way through the top piece. Countersink the holes and drive in screws to securely attach the two pieces of plywood together.

To cut the circular shape of the tabletop, the best method would be to use a router and a trammel device similar to what we used to draw the circle. There would be a pivot point at the center, but instead of a pencil at the outer end there would be a specialized mounting to hold a router. However, to do that requires a big beefy router and a long router bit – remember, the combined thickness of the two pieces of plywood is 1½". A little trim router won't do the job **(Photo 28)**.

Instead, use a jigsaw to cut thje circle. The jigsaw blade has teeth that cut upward, so wood tear-out and rough edges will be on the top surface of the workpiece. Because of this you'll want to make sure the top of the table is facing down so any tear-out will be on the bottom side of the table – this is why we drew the cut line for our circle on the underside of the bottom piece. *TIP – If your jigsaw has a setting for orbital action, set this as zero for the cleanest possible cut* **(Photo 29)**.

Work slow and steady as you cut. The jigsaw does a pretty good job at cutting out the circle, but it'll still need some clean up when you're done. You could use a block plane or rasp, but because plywood has multiple layers of wood going different directions, you're certain to get tear-out. So use an orbital sander to smooth the edges **(Photo 30)**.

When the sanding is done, place the legs on the bottom

of your tabletop. Position them so there is equal distance from the edge to each leg, then drill countersunk pilot holes and screw them down **(Photo 31)**.

The stain I chose was the Minwax Espresso color. I like the dark color, but it also helps hide any gaps there might be where the legs come together. And for the final clear finish I chose a brush-on lacquer. Lacquer is more clear where oil-based polyurethane has a slight yellow hue to it. Lacquer also dries very fast making it possible to apply multiple coats. Which is important if people will be placing their cold drinks on it.

Parts list in inches

QTY.	PART	THICKNESS	WIDTH	LENGTH
2	top halves*	$^3/_4$	36	36
3	legs**	$1^1/_2$	$4^1/_2$	36

*finished size, allow for cutting to size

**cut to width and length

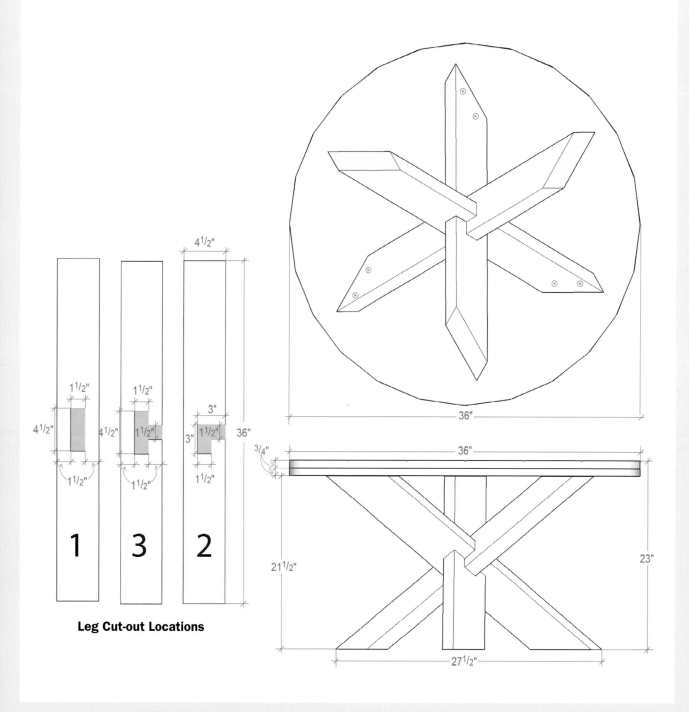

Leg Cut-out Locations

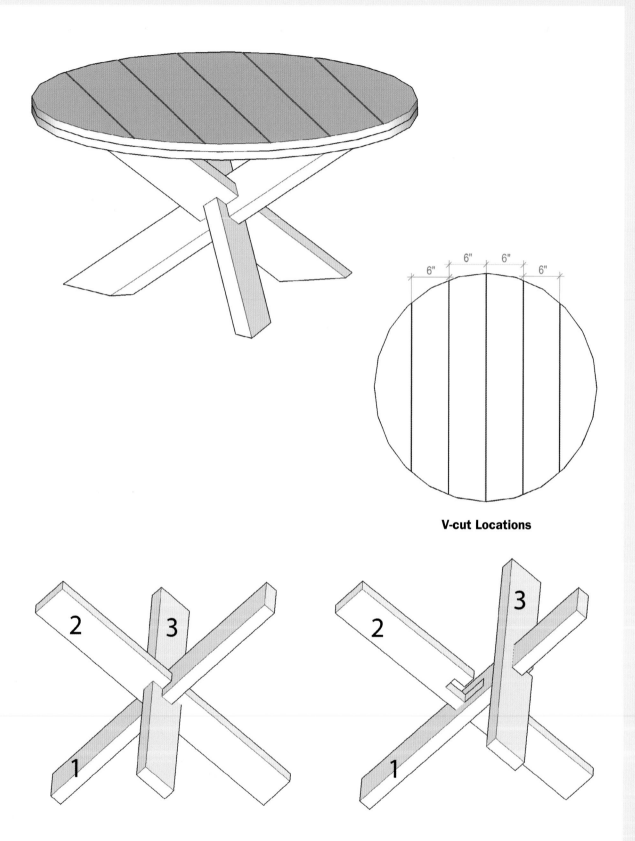

V-cut Locations

Base Assembly

Console Table

I just purchased a new flat-screen TV and it gave me the option to mount it to the wall. But mounting a flat screen TV to the wall limits my ability to rearrange the living room, so I decided to make a console table to set my TV on. After designing it, I realized it could easily be used as a sofa table or even as a desk. The contrasting woods and elegant curves really make this an eye-catching piece. Best of all, the construction is made with simple interlocking notches. Using a few basic tools and dimensional lumber you can complete this project in a weekend.

Begin this build by making the leg blocks that join the two legs together. The legs and blocks must have matching notches so the two workpieces will interlock **(Photo 1)**.

The legs blocks are made from a piece of 2x4. The 2x4 looks a little too wide for this table, so I cut them down to 2¹⁄₄" wide. It's easier and safer to rip a long board first with your jigsaw **(Photo 2)** and then cut the smaller blocks to length. Trying to hold and rip short little pieces can be dangerous.

Cut the blocks to the appropriate length. A miter saw is perfect for this. (Refer to the ICDT common rules for cutting multiple pieces on the miter saw).

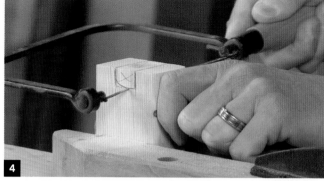

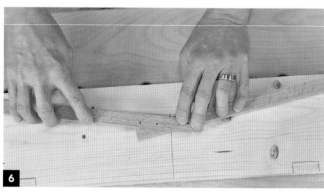

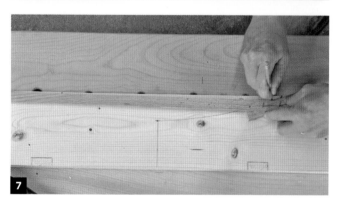

Using two thin strips of wood approximately 1/4" thick, position the strips so they touch the nails and overlap each other, then nail the strips together (Photo 6).

Remove the middle nail and place a pencil where the middle nail was. Keep pressure against the two nails and move the strips toward each end, and the strips magically create a nice smooth curve (Photo 7).

Once you've achieved a pleasing curve, cut it out with a jigsaw. Smooth out the resulting rough edge with a file or sandpaper.

Cut matching notches in the legs for the leg blocks to go into. Find the placement for the notches from the plans and cut them out with a jigsaw (Photo 8).

Test fit the leg blocks to the legs. If the fit is really tight, don't force it or hit it with a mallet or you could cause the leg block to split. Instead, file the block or leg notch until you get a firm but smooth fit. Then apply some glue, clamp it and set aside to dry (Photo 9). If the fit is too loose, don't panic – just drill a 1/16" pilot hole through the block and into the leg. Use glue and a 3d nail to set it in place.

With the leg sets done use the same process to form the long top stretchers. Again, from the plans, cut out the curves and notches in the correct locations.

The top is made up of two 1x10s glued together. Many times the factory edge is straight enough off the rack to join the two boards. Try placing the boards next to each other and look for the best fit with the seam having no gaps. If there is a gap, use a block plane and a combination square to true up the edge. Glue and clamp the top and set it aside to dry. (Refer to the ICDT common rules for clamping.)

With the leg blocks cut to length, cut notches for the 3/4"-thick legs to fit inside. The blocks are small and clamping them and using the jigsaw can be awkward and dangerous. So a better method is to place them in a vise and use a hand saw to cut the notches down to the proper depth (Photo 3). Then use a coping saw to cut across the grain to remove the rest of the waste (Photo 4).

It's better to cut the pieces a little too small versus too big – you can then sneak up on the line with a sharp chisel (Photo 5). Keep a scrap piece of 3/4" wood handy to test the openings after each cut to ensure a good snug fit.

The legs are made up of two 1x6s. Each leg has a curve on the outside edge you can create by making a template from the plans. However, if you choose to create your own curve you can do this with three nails and a thin strip of wood. To make your own curve, place a nail at the start and another nail at the end of the curve. Place a third nail in the middle at the height of the arc.

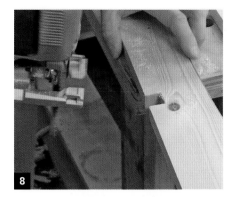

The top of the table is connected to three supports that interlock perpendicular to the stretcher by the use of notches. The three top supports are cut to length from a 1x4 per the cut list. Trace the curve onto the supports from the pattern provided in the plans, and use a jigsaw to cut out the curve. Make sure to sand the edges smooth. Cut out the notches the same way you did with the legs and test-fit the top support pieces. Again, if the top supports are too tight to fit together smoothly, sand or file them for a better fit. Do not hit them into place or the workpiece will break.

We'll attach the stretchers to the legs with pocket holes drilled at both ends of the stretchers. With the pocket hole jig still set up, also drill pocket holes at the ends of the lower shelf.

It's time for assembly! Begin by gluing the top supports into the stretchers **(Photo 10)**.

Attach the stretchers to the legs with pocket screws **(Photo 11)**.

NOTE – The clearance is only 6" so a short driver on your drill will be necessary. If you don't have a short driver, glue only the middle support to the stretcher. Attach stretchers to legs. Then glue other supports into the stretchers.

Then attach lower shelf **(Photo 12)**.

Turn the unit over and attach the other legs to the stretchers and lower shelf.

The top is attached with hardware called "figure-8 washers." These figure-8s look like two washers welded together. One hole allows a screw to go down into the top supports while the other hole allows a screw to go up into the underside of the top **(Photo 13)**.

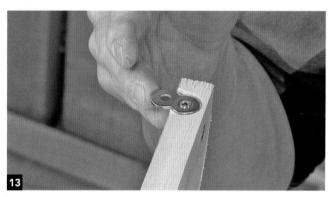

It'll look better if the washers sit flush with the top support. Use a 1/2" forstner bit and drill a shallow countersunk hole just deep enough to accomodate the thickness of the washer. The solid top needs to expand and contract through seasonal movements. To make sure the washer has freedom to move use a chisel to widen the countersunk hole. When attaching the screws they should be snug, but not too tight.

Place the tabletop on the workbench with the bottom facing upward. Turn the rest of the table upside down and place it onto the top. Measure equal distances from side to side and front to back, then screw the other half of the figure-8 washers to the underside of the tabletop.

After sanding, staining and finishing the complete piece to your liking, it's ready to become home to your TV.

Remember earlier when I noted that the design could work with other furniture? With just a few tweaks of a couple of key dimensions, you can use the same design to create a sofa table, end tables or even a desk.

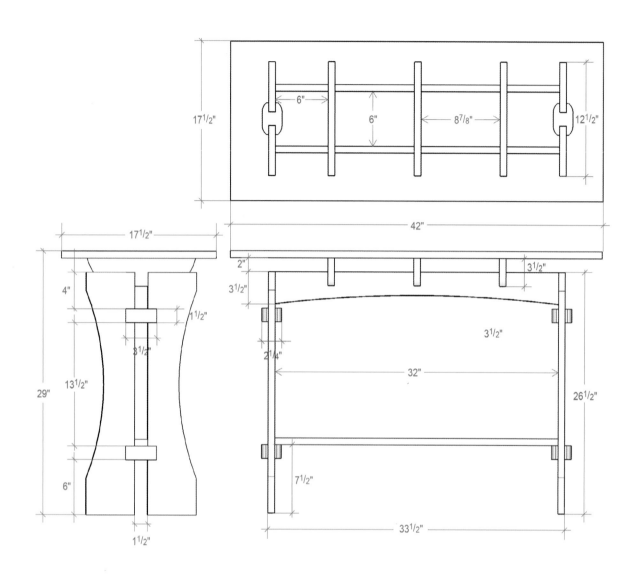

Parts list in inches

QTY.	PART	THICKNESS	WIDTH	LENGTH	NOTES
1	top	3/4	17 1/2	42	
4	legs	3/4	5 1/2	26 1/2	shape to pattern
4	leg blocks	1 1/2	2 1/4	3 1/2	shape to pattern
2	top stretchers	3/4	3 1/2	32	shape to pattern
3	top supports	3/4	3 1/2	12 1/2	shape to pattern
1	lower shelf	3/4	7 1/4	32	

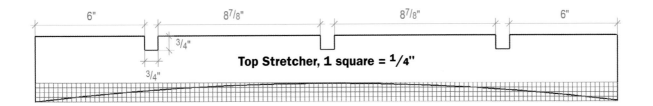

Top Stretcher, 1 square = $^1/_4$"

6" $8^7/_8$" $8^7/_8$"   6"

$3/_4$"

$3/_4$"

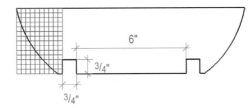

**Top Support,
1 square = $^1/_4$"**

6"

$3/_4$"

$3/_4$"

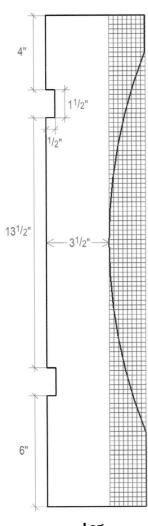

4"

$1^1/_2$"

$1/_2$"

$13^1/_2$"

$3^1/_2$"

6"

**Leg,
1 square = $^1/_4$"**

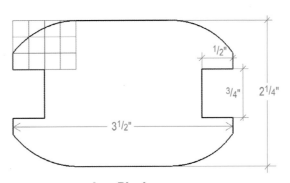

$1/_2$"

$3/_4$"

$2^1/_4$"

$3^1/_2$"

**Leg Block,
1 square = $^1/_4$"**

Pagoda End Table

When clamping the boards together, avoid using too much pressure. Excessive clamp pressure may cause the boards to crown, resulting in a cupped tabletop. A good rule of thumb is to add enough clamping pressure so that a small amount of glue squeeze-out is even across the joining edges (Photo 1).

While the top is in the clamps and drying, cut the tapered legs to length from 1x4s on the miter saw. Make sure the legs are all exactly the same length to avoid any wobble the table might have once completed. *TIP – Use a stop block on your miter saw to ensure the legs are the same length.*

Next, taper the legs. At the top of each leg, measure in 1¹/₄" from the edge. Use a yardstick or straightedge to draw a line extending from the the 1¹/₄" mark down to the bottom corner of the leg at the full width of the board. Pencil in an "X" on the waste side that will be cut off.

To cut the legs for the taper, use a jigsaw (Photo 2). It can be difficult to cut a perfectly straight line with a jigsaw, so when cutting the taper stay proud of the line and make sure to cut on the waste side of the cut line. Once the legs are cut out, mount the leg in a vise and use a block plane to shave down to the pencil line for a smooth, crisp edge.

These days, we seem to have a lot of gadgets around us. Cell phones, remote controls, tablets, laptops – you name it. Without them, many of us feel lost. So keeping them at arm's length has become a necessity. The perfect solution is a simple, but elegant, end table. This end table has a unique look and yet is simple to finish in a day. So the morning begins with a quick stop at the DIY store and then out to the shop to begin construction.

Because the tabletop is made up of two pieces of 1x8 glued together from narrower pieces, start there so the glue can dry while proceding with the rest of the steps. Using a circular saw and a clamped on straightedge cutting guide, crosscut the 1x8s to the proper length from the cut list.

Place the boards side-by-side to see how they fit. Make sure the joining edges have no gaps. If you see a gap, use a block plane and make a few light passes to square up the edges. Check the fit again and repeat the process if necessary. Once you've achieved a good fit apply a thin layer of glue to both edges of the boards and place in the clamps.

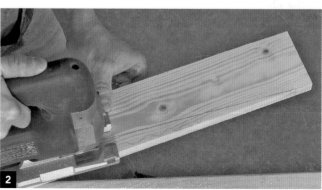

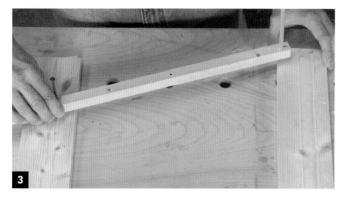

With the legs done, move on to the upper aprons and lower rails. These will also be made from 1x4 stock. On the miter saw, cut the aprons and rails to length according to the cut list. When first looking at the photos the upper aprons seem to be the same height as the lower rails. However, the lower rails have the shelf sitting on top of them. Keeping the lower rails the same height as the upper aprons would make the bottom look too thick, so cut 3/4" off the lower rails. Mark and draw a 3/4" line lengthwise on all the lower rails and cut off the waste with the jigsaw. Just like before, stay slightly proud of the line on the waste side and use a block plane to shave down to the line.

The aprons and lower rails have an arch to them, which you can create using a trammel. Trammels are nothing more than a long thin piece of wood, with a nail for a pivot point at one end and a pencil at the other end. The distance between the pivot point and pencil determines the radius of the circle to be drawn (Photo 3). You can create your own custom arch doing this, or simply use the pattern provided in the plans. Trace the arch onto the workpieces and cut them out with the jigsaw.

You can't use a block plane on a concave curve, of course. Instead, use a rasp to shave down to the line and frequently check to make sure the arch has a graceful, smooth curve to it. Then clean up the rough rasp marks with some sandpaper.

The vertical dowels on the table sides extend down through 3/8" holes in the upper side aprons. Measure and mark where the holes will go on the top edge of the side aprons per the plans. Then use a square to transfer the marks to the opposite curved edges. Drilling straight holes is essential for the dowels to go in properly. To achieve this, drill halfway through the workpiece, then turn it over and drill halfway the other direction to compete the hole (Photo 4). *TIP – To make a simple vise, clamp a wooden handscrew to the benchtop.*

Test fit your dowels to make sure they slide through the hole. Dowel rods are notoriously inconsistent in sizing and can also shrink or expand depending on climate changes. If the fit seems too tight, redrill the hole slightly oversized with a 13/32" drill bit. *TIP – If you don't have a 13/32" bit you can slightly enlarge the hole by pivoting back and forth with the 3/8" drill bit.*

Cut the bottom shelf to length from a 1x12. From the plans, mark the corners notches for the legs. Use a jigsaw to make these cuts, but take care and go slow to make nice, straight square cuts. This not only looks good, but also adds to the stability of the table (Photo 5).

The 3/8" dowels are set into holes drilled into the shelf. Measurements could be taken and laid out from the plans, but a nifty trick is to just use the upper curved apron as a guide. Place the flat edge of the apron onto the shelf in between the leg notches. Slide a 3/8" drill bit down into each hole and press down on the bit to make a mark on the shelf (Photo 6).

Set the apron aside and drill the holes all the way through the shelf on your marks. Make sure to have a sacrificial board beneath your workpiece so you don't drill into the workbench.

To begin assembly, drill horizontal pocket holes into the

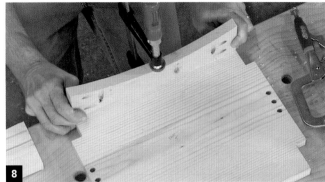

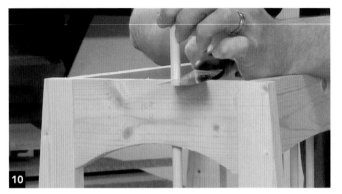

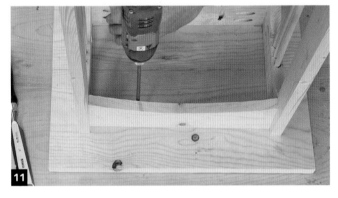

to the rest of the assembly (Photo 9).

Slide the dowels from the top down through the aprons and into the lower shelf. Use a flush cutting saw and trim the dowels so they're flush with the apron (Photo 10).

Before attaching the top, the pocket holes we drilled earlier on the upper aprons should be elongated a bit. Since the top is solid wood it will expand and contract with the season changes, and enlarging the holes will allow for a bit of seasonal movement.

Pocket holes are "stepped" with a wider countersunk opening at the top that contains the screw head, and a thinner hole for the screw's threaded shank. It's this thinner hole we want to elongate.

Use a drill bit that matches the size of this thinner hole, and insert it into the hole. Fire up the drill and rock the bit back and forth to elongate the opening side-to-side. You don't need a lot of wiggle room, maybe just an additional 1/8" on each side of the hole. The alignment of the elongated hole should go perpendicular to the apron thickness.

Place the top on the workbench with the bottom of it facing up. Turn the rest of the project upside down and place it on the top and measure equal distance from both front and back and side-to-side. Now screw the assembly to the top. Don't use any glue so the top can move freely with seasonal changes (Photo 11).

As with any project, sanding, staining and finish are the final touches.

Once this end table is finished, it can be placed by your sofa or bed – or really anywhere in the home you leave your "stuff."

ends of the upper aprons and lower rails. Also drill some vertical pocket holes on the front and back aprons you'll use later to attach the top.

The assembly is straightforward at this point, but the following procedure will help avoid frustration during this process.

Attach the legs to the side rails and aprons first. This order is important because failing to do so will result in insufficient room to get the drill inside to attach the sides later. Use some glue on the ends of the rails and aprons and then clamp the pieces flat to fasten them with pocket screws to the legs (Photo 7).

With the side units assembled, attach only the upper aprons. We'll attach the lower front and back rails to the shelf before mounting it to the legs (Photo 8).

Glue and screw the lower rails to the shelf. The rails should sit flush with the edges of the shelf. Having the shelf and rails out and free from the rest of the project makes it easier to plane or sand flush if needed. Now glue and screw the shelf and rails

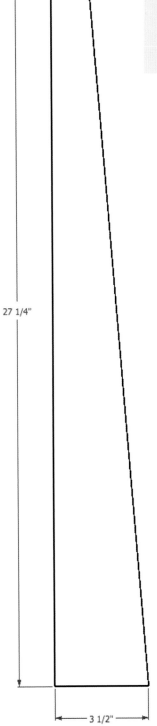

Parts list in inches

QTY.	PART	THICKNESS	WIDTH	LENGTH	NOTES
1	top	$3/4$	$14^1/2$	18	
1	shelf	$3/4$	$11^1/4$	$12^1/2$	corners notched
4	legs	$3/4$	$3^1/2$	$27^1/4$	shaped to template
2	long upper stretchers	$3/4$	$3^1/2$	$12^1/2$	shaped to template
2	long lower stretchers	$3/4$	$2^3/4$	$12^1/2$	shaped to template
2	short upper stretchers	$3/4$	$3^1/2$	7	shaped to template
2	short lower stretchers	$3/4$	$2^3/4$	7	shaped to template
6	dowels	$3/8$	$3/8$	17	

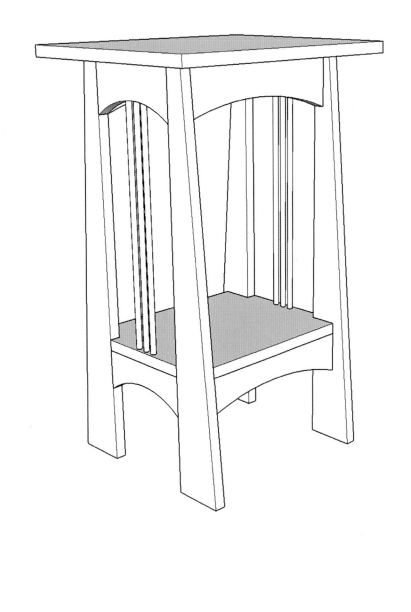

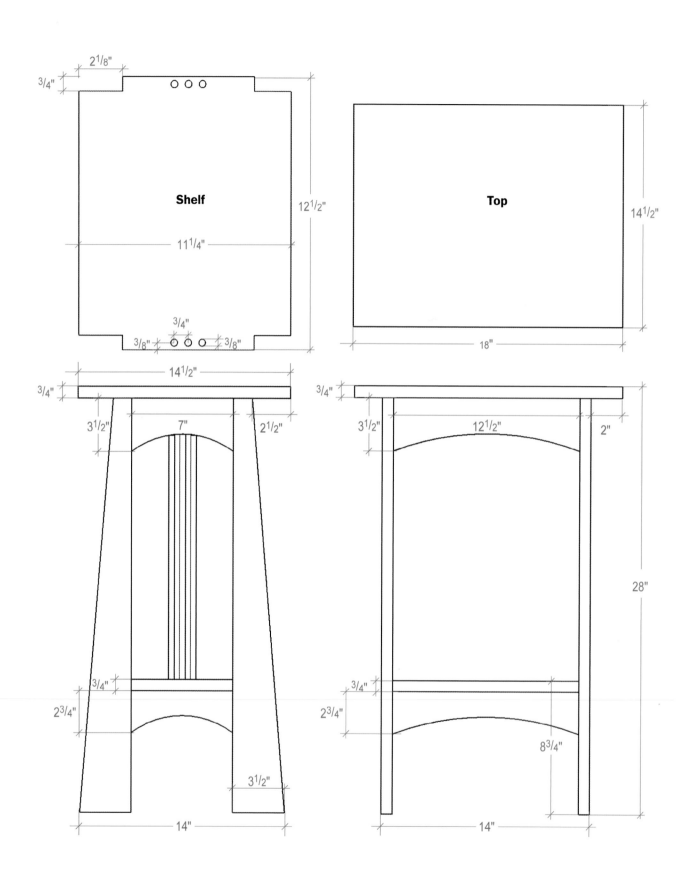

Shelf

2 1/8"
3/4"
12 1/2"
11 1/4"
3/4"
3/8"
3/8"

Top

14 1/2"
18"

14 1/2"
3/4"
3 1/2"
7"
2 1/2"
3/4"
2 3/4"
3 1/2"
14"

3/4"
3 1/2"
12 1/2"
2"
28"
3/4"
2 3/4"
8 3/4"
14"

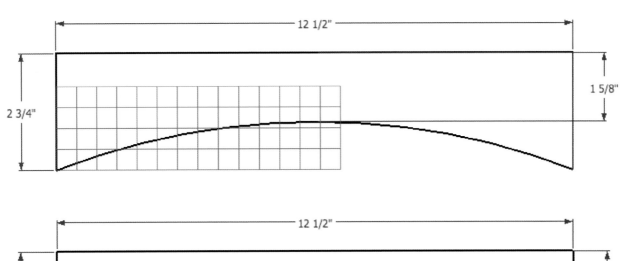

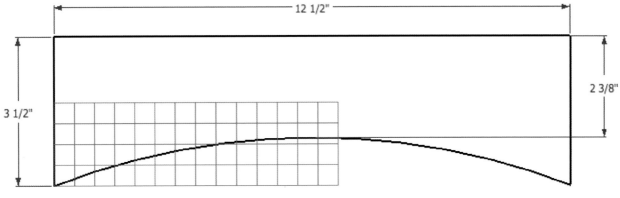

1 square = 1/2"

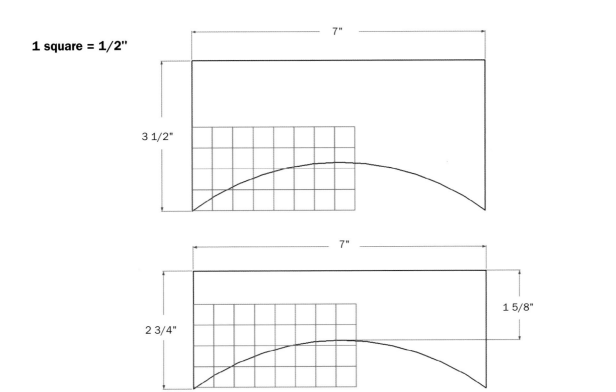

Table for Two

Summertime! For most folks summertime conjures up thoughts of holidays, parties, and frequent cookouts. But all of these occasions require plenty of seating for the guests, and even if you have a picnic table or full set of otudoor furniture there are times when you still need a few more places for people to sit and eat. Some easy-to-store extra seating sure could save the day.

Then there are the times when you head for a cookout at the local park or go camping in places with no picnic tables. Wouldn't it be great to have a small table and chairs you could toss in the car?

You've got both of those scenarios covered with this project. Made from basic dimensional lumber, this small table set is quick to make and folds up for easy transport, or for storage when not in use. The table has slightly larger dimensions than the seats, but the construction is exactly the same. For this project we'll just make one set, but make as many as you'd like (and start inviting more people to your cookouts).

Begin by cutting some 1x4 stock to make the legs and cleats for the seats. Each seat requires four legs and four cleats, so rip enough 1¾" material to cover the needed lengths per the cut list.

Find the middle of a board and draw a line lengthwise to rip the board in half. This step is an easy job for a table saw,

however a jigsaw can do the job. Take time and go slow to cut right on your cut line to create two equal halves. Once ripped in two, use a block plane to smooth and clean up the saw marks. Each workpiece will be approximately 1¾" in width after cutting **(Photo 1)**. *NOTE – Because the saw kerf and planing removes a bit of material when cutting the 1x4, the actual width will be slightly less than 1¾". But don't worry, as long as they're all equal this won't affect the project assembly in any way.*

Use a miter saw or handsaw to cut the four leg pieces and seat cleats to length.

For the seats to fold open and closed, the legs must be accurately measured and drilled to create the pivot points.

Find and mark the middle of a workpiece with a combination square. Measure the distance to the mark and set the square, then use it to make a mark the same distance from one end of each piece. Repeat the process for all four legs and cleats **(Photo 2)**.

Lay the legs side-by-side on your bench and measure from end-to-end to find the center. Use the square to mark across all four legs **(Photo 3)**. Now, mark the center of the line on each individual leg to mark the drilling spot.

The legs and seat cleats are curved on the ends to allow smooth operation when opened and closed. Set a compass to half the width of the leg workpieces and place it on the bolt

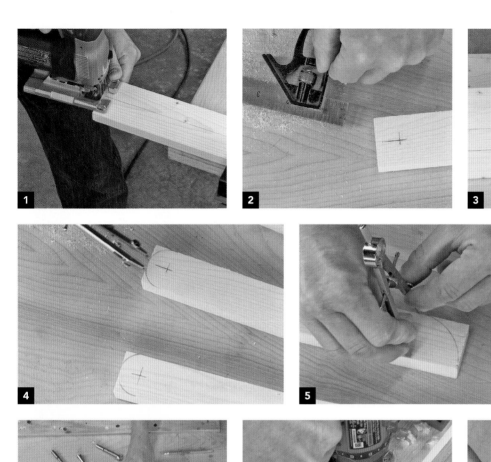

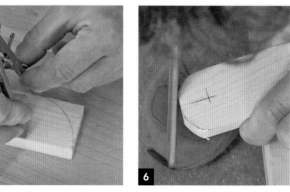

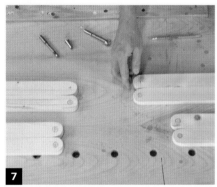

placement mark at one end of each leg and form a half circle radius. This will be the leg top **(Photo 4)**.

For the bottom of the legs, and on both ends of the seat cleats, reset the compass to the full width of the leg and form a quarter circle radius **(Photo 5)**.

Cut these curves with a jigsaw. If the curve is too tight to stay exactly on the line, cut a series of straight lines just proud of the radius pencil line. Then you can easily shape to the line with a sander or file **(Photo 6)**.

Although all your hole marks on the legs and cleats are drilled for the bolts to go though, certain sides have to be countersunk so a nut or bolt head won't interfere with the pivoting action. Likewise, we'll countersink the outer visible holes for a clean appearance. Keep in mind, there are not only individual left and right legs but there are also left and right leg assemblies. The placement of the countersunk holes is crucial for the proper assembly of the legs. Refer to the drawing diagram, and lay out the pieces for each side and circle which holes are countersunk **(Photo 7)**.

Use a ⁷/₈" Forstner bit to make the countersink. You could also use a spade (or paddle) bit, but a Forstner bit makes a much cleaner cut. Make the countersink approximately ¹/₂" deep. Verify that the countersink is deep enough by placing the head of the bolt and nut in it and make sure all bolt heads and nuts are below the face of the board. Drill ³/₈" clearance holes in the center of each countersink to allow the bolts to go through.

To prevent drilling into your bench or work surface, place a scrap piece of wood under your workpiece **(Photo 8)**.

Assemble the legs in pairs. Once assembled, each pair of leg assemblies should mirror each other. Use ³/₈" fender washers behind the nut and bolt and also between each leg pair. *TIP – If you plan to leave your folding seats outside, use stainless steel or galvanized hardware.*

It's important that the nut doesn't come loose over time with the operation of the opening and closing. To assure this, the nut must be locked into place. There are several items on the market that will do this, like locking washers

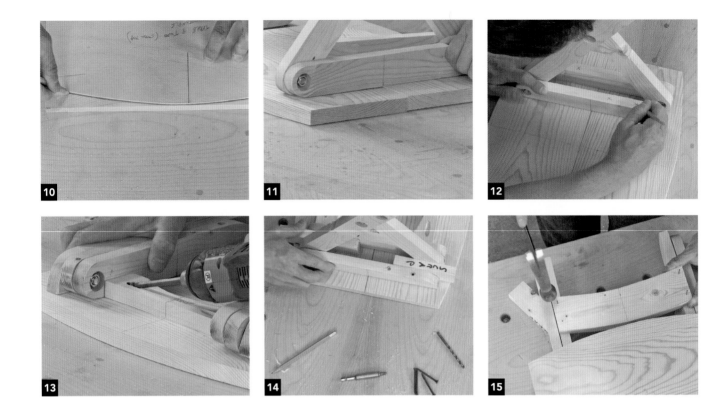

and locknuts. But both are too thick and would cause the nut to stand out higher than the face of the board. Instead, use a product called "thread lock," a liquid that can be applied to the threads of the bolt and once it dries it firmly holds the nut in place **(Photo 9)**.

Connecting the two pairs of leg assemblies is done with the handle, brace and lower stretchers.

The stretchers are different lengths but have the same curve on them. From the plans, make a template that you can trace onto the stretchers **(Photo 10)**.

Cut the stretchers out with a jigsaw and smooth the rough edges. We'll glue and face-nail them to the legs later, but set them aside for now.

The handle and brace are the same length, but the handle has a slight curve to it, cut with a jigsaw. Each piece is drilled with a pocket hole bit, and then glued and screwed to the legs when it's time for assembly.

The seat has a nice curve to it. Using the same template for the curve on the stretchers, draw the curve on the two seat pieces, then cut it out with the jigsaw and smooth the edges.

Final assembly is the most important step. With the leg assembly upside down, place it on the two halves of the seat. The center of the leg cleats should line up where the edges of the two seat pieces come together **(Photo 11)**.

Mark the cleat for two countersunk 3/8" holes and two 3/16" clearance holes on the toe end of each seat cleat. It is important the holes for the screws are on the proper side of the cleat. If screws are attached on the wrong end, the seat will not open **(Photo 12)**.

Begin assembly by gluing and screwing the handle and

brace to each pair of leg assemblies **(Photo 13)**.

Making sure the legs fold up without binding or pinching is essential for this seat to work. Use scrap pieces of wood the same thickness as the legs, and temporarily clamp them between the cleat and legs. Use a 2" screw and attach the cleat to the seat **(Photo 14)**.

With the screws in place, remove the scrap spacers and test the opening and closing of the seat. The last thing to attach are the stretchers. Close the seat into it's folded position and lay it on the workbench.

Drill 1/16" pilot holes in each stretcher, then glue and nail the stretchers in place with 11/4" 3d nails **(Photo 15)**. Note which stretchers go on the correct legs. Failure to do so will prevent the seat from opening.

This completes the seat – which is great practice for making the slightly larger table since it's built the same way, just with the material supersized.

The usual sanding steps are required before applying any finish to it, but the correct finish is important on this project. The legs have a tight tolerance, and for this reason paint or a thick top coat like polyurethane is not recommended. It could interfere with a smoot-moving action during opening and closing. For interior use, stain and a wipe-on poly or Danish oil can be used. For an exterior finish, try a 50/50 mixture of boiled linseed oil and mineral spirits. These types of finishes soak into the wood more that a regular polyurethane, which builds up layers on the surface of the wood.

The table for two is complete and the only thing missing is a good friend to come over for a cookout. And now that you have more seating, be sure to invite several.

Parts list in inches

QTY.	PART	THICKNESS	WIDTH	LENGTH	NOTES
TABLE					
4	legs	3/4	3½	30	shaped one end
4	leg cleats	3/4	3½	16	shaped both ends
1	leg stretcher	3/4	3½	18½	shape to pattern
1	leg stretcher	3/4	3½	17	shape to pattern
2	handle and brace	3/4	3½	14	shape to pattern
2	top halves	3/4	14	28	glued up/shape to pattern
STOOLS (for 2)					
8	legs	3/4	11 1/16*	20	*width determined when ripping
8	leg cleats	3/4	11 1/16	11½	shaped both ends
2	leg stretcher	3/4	11 1/16	12	shape to pattern
2	leg stretcher	3/4	11 1/16	10¼	shape to pattern
4	handle and brace	3/4	11 1/16	7½	shape to pattern
4	seat halves	3/4	7¼	16	shape to pattern
HARDWARE (for table and 2 stools)					
18	bolts	3/8		1¼	
36	fender washers	3/8			
18	nuts	3/8			

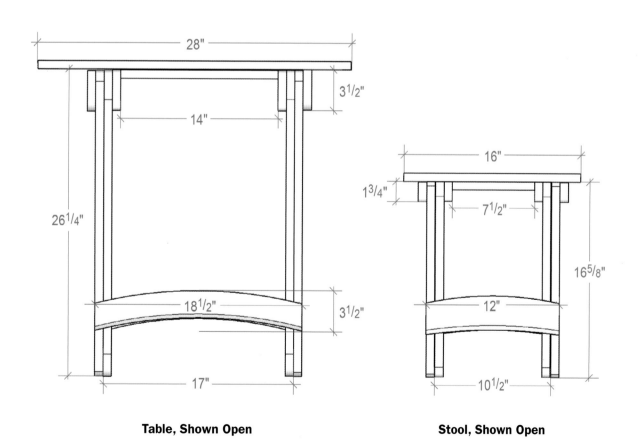

Table, Shown Open

Stool, Shown Open

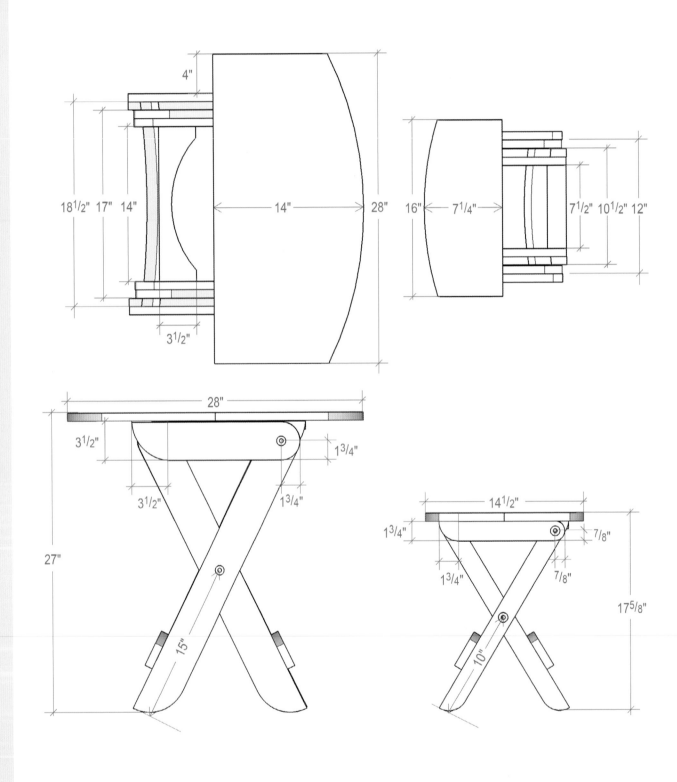

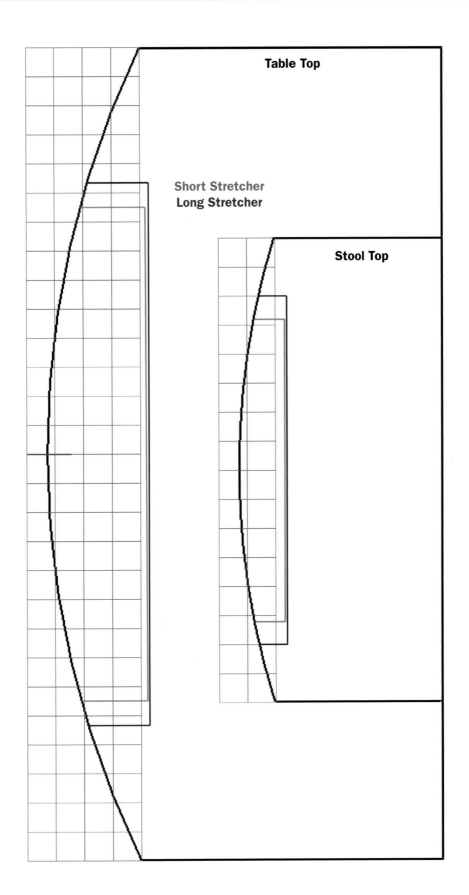

Table Top

Short Stretcher
Long Stretcher

Stool Top

1 square = 1"

Picnic Table

Living in the Midwest we get all of the extreme weather changes from the four seasons. So when a nice, warm spring day comes around, I like to take advantage of it. When I think of a perfect day, I think of a picnic. And of course, what's a picnic without a picnic table?

Most picnic tables are of the long rectangular design. A typical picnic table can accommodate six people, but usually only about four people will use it. I wanted a different design because most people don't like sitting in the middle. Plus, many times such picnic tables have attached benches which can be awkward; you have to climb in and out of them. Not to mention that when it's time to mow the grass you have to move the whole structure – and that gets heavy. So this design is octagonal in shape, and with four separate smaller benches it's easy to move the table wherever you want it.

Picnic tables are typically made of pressure-treated lumber because they are most likely left outdoors year round. Pressure-treated lumber is wood infused with chemicals to help prevent decay and insects. However, this chemical process tends to warp the wood and cause cracks as the wood ages. I believe a better option is to buy regular lumber and treat it with an exterior deck stain. But first, the key to any solid, well-made table is to select good, straight lumber.

When choosing lumber look for pieces that are straight and not cupped, bowed, crooked or twisted. And if the wood is still damp, try to find the driest boards. Once the lumber is selected, it's time to start building.

From the plans, cut the three middle boards for the tabletop to length. Use some 3/16" scraps in between each board for spacing, and measure the combined width of the three boards. This will give the length of the boards for the octagonal frame to go around the outside edge of the table. *TIP – It's better to measure the actual boards versus the measurements on the plans because the wood from the lumber store might be slightly oversized or undersized.* **(Photo 1)**

Making the outer octagonal frame means cutting the angles at 22$\frac{1}{2}$° on the miter saw. Make one cut on the end of the board at 22$\frac{1}{2}$° and then measure over from the bottom edge and mark for the opposing angle. *TIP – It can be difficult to hook the end of a tape measure on the heel of the mitered board. The tape measure will have the tendency to slip off. A better way is to hang the tape measure over the edge to start at the 1" mark. But make sure to add 1" to your overall length before marking the board.* **(Photo 2)**

Instead of measuring each piece, use the first one as a template for marking the others.

We'll join the mitered pieces to form the entire octagon with exterior 2$\frac{1}{2}$" pocket screws, but first do a partial assembly to double-check the fit. To do this, create two partial "halves" by connecting just three of the pieces for each side. Now, clamp these to your bench with a loose seventh piece in place at one end **(Photo 3)**. Sometimes, the last piece will either be too big or too small. In this case, the piece came out too small.

Several things could have caused this. For example, if

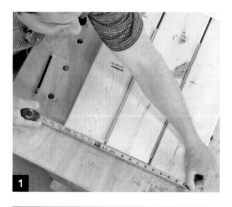

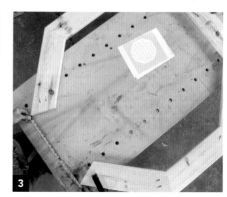

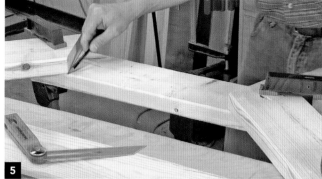

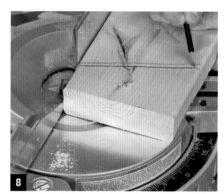

the miter saw was off just a slight fraction of a degree, the problem is compounded 16 times because of all the miter cuts. Another issue that could cause the problem is if each board is not cut at the exact length – simply cutting on the wrong side of the pencil line can result in the same problem.

The simple fix is to just cut the last piece to the size needed. But I want the table to be as symmetrical as possible with each piece the same length. So here is the solution.

The table should be 50$\frac{1}{2}$" in length and width. Cut to length and place the middle tabletop boards in position, using a long clamp to hold them securely (Photo 4).

Each end of the table has a missing piece. Clamp a longer piece of 2x6 to the bottom of the octagonal frame bridging the space of the missing pieces. Trace pencil lines onto the 2x6 at the ends of the miters (Photo 5).

Once the pencil lines are traced, the angle of the lines have to be figured out. I know it's not 22$\frac{1}{2}$" because my pieces didn't fit exactly. I could use an angle finder gauge, but I have the same issue with the angle finders as I do my saw; I have to trust that the gauge is accurate and that it's calibrated to my saw. A better way to do this is with a bevel gauge.

Remove the 2x6 from the clamps and place the bevel gauge on the board. Keep the handle of the bevel against the edge of the 2x6 and line up the blade with the pencil line (Photo 6).

Lock the bevel in place and then take it to the miter saw. Keep the handle of the bevel flat against the fence of the miter saw. Turn the table of the miter saw to line up with the angle of the blade on the bevel gauge (Photo 7). Lock the miter saw in place, but don't make the actual cut yet. With the 2x6 on the miter saw, make a shallow practice cut on the waste side of the board. Check to see if the practice cut is

perfectly parallel to the pencil line. In this case, you can see the saw's table has to be slightly adjusted. (Photo 8).

Repeat this process until the fine adjusting of the miter saw is achieved and then make the cut. NOTE – You have to do this same process for both sides of the workpiece.

Once accomplished, the workpiece will fit perfectly into place and be the same length as all of the other eight pieces (Photo 9). Now drill and drive pocket screws to hold the workpiece in place, completing the octagonal frame.

Cut the remaining tabletop pieces to fit inside your octagon. Use some scrap pieces of 2x6 and cut them at 45° on the miter saw. With the same $\frac{3}{16}$" spacers, make sure that the 2x6s fit in the remaining space. It might be necessary to shave some width off the last board (Photo 10).

Measure the length needed to fit the 2x6 in place. Mark the 2x6 but cut proud of the line, making the board a little long. Slowly sneak up on the line and test the fit of the board in the tabletop until a nice fit is achieved. Then pocket-screw it in place.

Set the top aside and start constructing the legs. Measure

from the cut list the length of the legs and make the cuts at 45° **(Photo 11)**.

Once the legs are cut to the same length, find the center of the legs. Drill a pilot hole through the center of one of the legs. *TIP – To help drill a hole straight through the board, drill half way then turn the board over and drill the other half.*

Place a 2½" pocket screw through the pilot hole. Line the screw up with the center of the other leg. Drive the screw through into the second leg forming a pivot point. Stand the legs up so the feet are flush with the workbench.

When the bases of the legs are flat, place two more screws through the legs to hold this position **(Photo 12)**.

Construct a second pair of legs in the same manner. The two leg sets are joined with a stretcher, so first lay out the placement for the stretcher. Use the square at a 45° angle and find the center of where the two legs intersect **(Photo 13)**. From that center line measure over ¾" on both sides of it **(Photo 14)**.

Place a scrap piece of 2x6 between the lines and then center it from top to bottom. Then trace around the 2x6 to mark the stretcher's mounting location **(Photo 15)**.

Drill two countersunk clearance holes through the leg sets to allow ½" x 5" lags screws to go through. Also, back out each pocket screw one at a time and countersink the hole to allow the screws to set a bit deeper. *NOTE – Make sure to drill pilot holes into the stretcher ends before tightening the lag screws, otherwise the stretcher may split.*

Upend the leg assembly onto the underside of the tabletop. Measure equal distance from the edge to the legs so they are evenly placed. Attach some 2x2 stock to the legs with a couple of carriage screws and nuts driven horizontally to the tabletop. Then, secure the leg assembly with lag screws vertically through the 2x2 and into the underside of the tabletop **(Photo 16)**.

TIP – Because the picnic table will be sitting outside in all weather conditions moisture is an issue. The legs resting on the ground are endgrain. Endgrain will soak up water like a sponge. Water inside the wood will cause premature damage. So to help prevent this, apply a thin layer of exterior glue to the bottom edges of the legs to help seal it.

With the table complete, let's start on the bench seats. Again, most tables have attached benches, but these separate benches are easily moved and stored away for winter.

The bench legs are made from 2x4s, but the seats themselves are assembled from a pair of 2x8s that have a smooth arc both front and back. Create these with a template made from 1/4" plywood and an arc-drawing jig. This jig essentially looks and acts like a bow and arrow. To make one, start with a narrow length of 1/4" wood with holes at each end, and tie string from one hole to the other to form the "bow." A shorter length of wood with notches cut into one end is the "arrow." Place the arrow into the bow, looping the string through the notches to stretch the bow into an arc. The shape of the arc is determined by the notch the string is in – the farther the notch is from the bow, the tighter the arc **(Photo 17)**. Trace the arc on each side of the template, then cut it out with a jigsaw.

Now, place the template on the 2x8s, trace the pattern

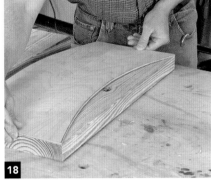

onto the two pieces of 2x8 making up the seat, and cut out with the jigsaw **(Photo 18)**.

The bench legs are constructed in the same fashion as the legs on the table. However, there are a couple of changes. The legs were cut at 45° on the miter saw, but cutting the bench legs at 45° would have had the legs extend too far out past the seat making it a tripping hazard. Cutting them less than 30° would make them unstable and the bench could easily tip over. We chose 30° and made the second change, moving the intersection higher on the legs. By moving the screw location from the center of the legs, it creates a leg set that is narrower at the top **(Photo 19)**.

As with the table, a stretcher joins the two leg sets together and is attached in the same manner as the table legs. A countersunk hole, clearance hole, pilot hole into the stretcher and then the lag screw are tightened up **(Photo 20)**.

Place the narrow end of the leg assembly upside-down onto the inverted seat. Center the legs and then trace around them onto the underside of the seat boards.

To attach the seat boards, return the leg assembly right-side up. Now, use a clamp and some 3/16" scrap as a spacer in between them to keep the seat together, and place it atop the leg assembly. When drilling the pilot holes for the screws, drill on the same angle as the legs so the screws go into the leg parallel to get maximum strength and avoid splitting the leg **(Photo 21)**.

The screws we're using are weatherproof 2¹/₂" deck screws. These have self-taping threads at the tip, followed by regular threads on the shank. At the top of the screws

are reverse threads that help prevent the board from mushrooming. To top it off, these screws have narrow Torx heads that are almost unnoticeable when in place **(Photo 22)**.

Drive the screws completely in so they are below the surface of the seat.

With the first bench done, make three more just like it.

The finising touch is to add some protection and enhance the beauty. Your best bet is an all-in-one deck stain that has both color and a sealant **(Photo 23)**.

Apply the coating per the instructions on the can, and allow to dry thoroughly. After that, the only thing left is to have some friends over for a nice cookout.

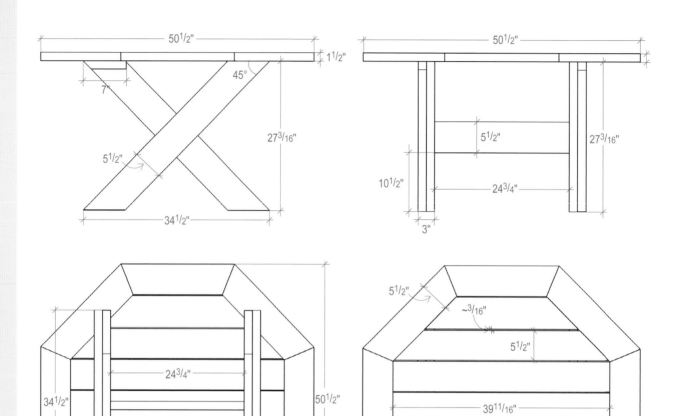

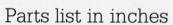

Parts list in inches

QTY.	PART	THICKNESS	WIDTH	LENGTH
5	top slats	$1^1/_2$	$5^1/_2$	$39^{11}/_{16}$
2	top slats	$1^1/_2$	$5^1/_2$	$28^1/_2$*
8	top border pieces	$1^1/_2$	$5^1/_2$	$21^1/_8$*
4	legs**	$1^1/_2$	$5^1/_2$	43
1	stretcher	$1^1/_2$	$5^1/_2$	$24^3/_4$
4	mounting blocks	$1^1/_2$	$1^1/_2$	7
4	6" x $^1/_4$" lag bolts w/ washers			
8	3" x $^1/_4$" carriage bolts			

*cut to fit

**45° angle both ends

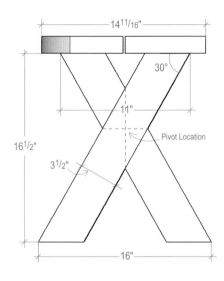

14^{11}/$_{16}$"
30°
11"
16^{1}/$_{2}$"
3^{1}/$_{2}$"
Pivot Location
16"

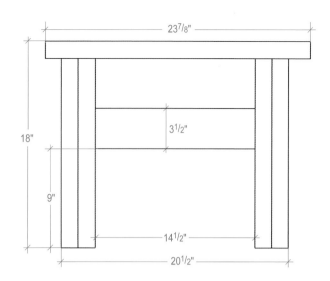

23^{7}/$_{8}$"
18"
3^{1}/$_{2}$"
9"
14^{1}/$_{2}$"
20^{1}/$_{2}$"

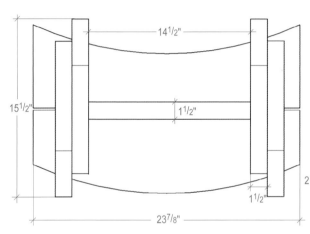

14^{1}/$_{2}$"
15^{1}/$_{2}$"
1^{1}/$_{2}$"
1^{1}/$_{2}$"
23^{7}/$_{8}$"

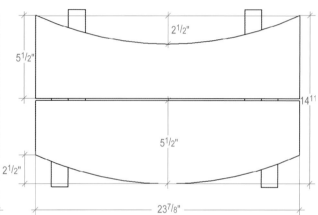

2^{1}/$_{2}$"
5^{1}/$_{2}$"
14^{11}
5^{1}/$_{2}$"
2^{1}/$_{2}$"
23^{7}/$_{8}$"

Parts list in inches (for 4 benches)

QTY.	PART	THICKNESS	WIDTH	LENGTH
8	seat halves*	1^{1}/$_{2}$	7^{1}/$_{4}$	23^{7}/$_{8}$
16	legs**	1^{1}/$_{2}$	3^{1}/$_{2}$	22
4	stretcher	1^{1}/$_{2}$	3^{1}/$_{2}$	14^{1}/$_{2}$
16	6" x ^{1}/$_{4}$" lag bolts w/ washers			

*cut to pattern

**30° angle both ends

Hallway Bench

To state the obvious, a hallway bench is an ideal place to sit to put on your shoes. You'll love having one for dealing with boots in the wintertime. But this handsome bench is not limited to just the foyer. It works well in the living room as a TV console or even as a coffee table.

It has two drawers for storage and a lower shelf to store items off the floor. This bench does incorporate some solid oak, but it's mostly made out of oak-veneered plywood. Plywood is comprised of multiple thin layers of wood glued and stacked on top of each other alternating the grain orientation with each layer. This alternating grain direction makes the wood very stable from seasonal movements and much more affordable than solid wood. However, the actual top layer of the plywood (in this case, oak) is only 1/32" thick, so keep in mind that the surface can damage easily.

Before buying plywood, inspect it just like you would regular lumber. When it comes to plywood types, a whole book could be written on that. But in general, plywood is graded with A,B,C or D. ("A" being the best and "D" a lesser quality) or graded as Premium, Cabinet Grade, Good 1 Side, and Shop Grade. The better the plywood the nicer the grain pattern and the fewer the defects. For the most part, the Big box stores have B or C grade plywood. Meaning it will have a decent grain pattern on one side while the other side could have minor flaws such as knot holes, mineral streaks or areas with filler in it. Look for plywood that is not bowed, or has the inner layers and glue separating. At least one side should look decent and clean.

Once you have the plywood back in the shop, place it on your workbench with some sacrificial boards underneath it. Before cutting plywood pay attention to the rotation of the saw blade. As the blade exits the wood it will cause minor splintering or tear-out. This splintering is best kept

on the bottom side of the finished project. With a circular saw the blade rotates such that the teeth come up through the workpiece, which can create tear-out on the top surface. To counter that, the good or finished surface side of the plywood should always face down when cutting with a circular saw. However, if you're cutting it on a table saw, the opposite applies – a table saw's blade rotates such that the teeth exit the workpiece going down, so the good or finished surface should face up.

Here are some tips to help minimize tear-out on the plywood.

- Apply tape to the wood first. Draw the cut line on the tape and then make the cut right through the tape. The tape helps hold pressure to the wood as the blade exits, thereby minimizing the tear-out.
- Score the wood on the cut line with a sharp knife. This cuts the wood fibers on the plywood and reduces the tear-out. To do this, adjust the saw to make a shallow cut that only goes between 1/16" and 1/8" into the plywood. This is called a score cut. Then reset the blade depth to make a deeper second cut through the rest of the wood.

Whichever method you use still requires a straight cut. You can build a simple jig for the circular saw that makes accurate straight cuts. The jig has a fence for the saw edge to guide against while the base of the jig is in exact alignment with the blade.

Once you've drawn a cut line on the plywood, place the jig right on the line, clamp it to the workpiece and make the cut (Photo 1).

The plywood will yield the top, shelves, sides, drawer dividers, and back rail for the hallway bench by following the sizes and measurements from the cut list. Once the pieces are cut, begin with the middle shelf and drill pilot holes in the ends to attach the dividers (Photo 2).

Besides the pilot holes for the dividers, this shelf, and the bottom shelf, receives pocket holes on the ends to attach the sides later (Photo 3).

Glue and attach the back rail and dividers to the middle shelf piece with screws (Photo 4).

After the back rail is on, the drawer dividers are next. But before screwing the dividers in place, double-check that they're square with the back rail. These dividers will help guide the drawers, so if they're out-of-square the drawer can be too loose, or may bind and get stuck (Photo 5).

With the three drawer dividers all in place, the middle

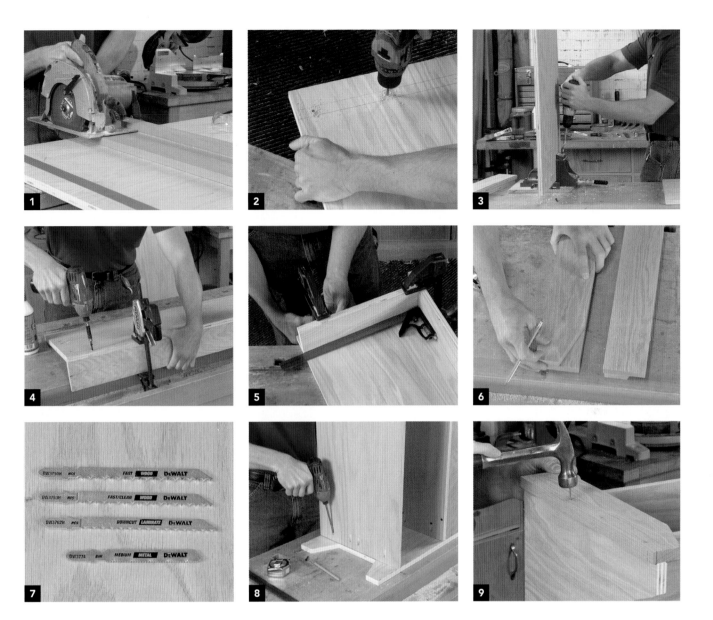

shelf unit is done and can be set aside.

The legs are cut from solid oak 1x4, while the sides are another piece of plywood. From the plans cut the angle for the foot of the leg and then cut the plywood sides. *TIP – cut one leg and then use that as a template for the other legs and sides (Photo 6).*)

A jigsaw can be used to cut out the shape, but before using the jigsaw choose the right blade for the task.

When choosing a jigsaw blade, pay attention to the direction and number of teeth. Blades have either "up-cut" or "down-cut" teeth. The direction of the teeth is vital to know because it determines which side the splintering or tear-out may occur. Also, the fewer the teeth, the faster the cut – but also the rougher the final finish will be **(Photo 7)**. More teeth on the blade results in a slower cut, but smoother finish. After making the cuts, clean up any edges with saw marks or rough edges using a block plane or file.

Also, if your jigsaw has a setting for orbital action – which angles the blade into the cut on the up stroke – set this to zero for the smoothest cut.

Keep the inside of the workpiece facing up while cutting with an upcut blade.

With the legs cut and cleaned up, attach the middle shelf unit to one of the sides with pocket screws **(Photo 8)**. Attach the lower shelf to the same side with pocket screws. Now, flip the assembly over to attach the opposite side in the same manner, and the basic carcase is done and ready for the legs.

The legs have a 1/4" reveal from the side. To keep this reveal consistent all the way down the side, make a pencil mark on the top and bottom of the leg to offset it from the side piece, then glue and nail the legs to the carcase **(Photo 9)**.

As you're creating the side reveal, make sure that the inside edge of the leg is flush with the drawer divider so the drawer can slide easily.

Using the same procedure, attach the other three legs in the same manner.

Make the drawers before putting the top on the bench.

Having the top off gives easier access to the drawer opening for measurements and checking the fit.

The drawers are made from 1/2" plywood. From the cut list, use a circular saw to rip the plywood to the height and then crosscut the sides to length on the miter saw. The lengths for the drawer front and back should be taken right from the bench. If the middle divider is slightly off to one side or the other the length of the front and back pieces will change.

To get an accurate measurement of the length of each front and back, place the side pieces together inside the drawer space. Then with a tape measure, measure the distance from the side pieces to the divider **(Photo 10)**.

Test fit the front and back pieces in the drawer opening before assembling the drawer. Once a nice fit is achieved, glue and nail the drawer together.

The bottom of each drawer is also 1/2" plywood and fits inside the drawer frame. First make sure the corner edge of the drawer is square. Then place the drawer on the plywood fitting one corner of the plywood lightly inside the corner of the drawer. Then trace the opposite corner onto the plywood **(Photo 11)** and cut the plywood with a jigsaw. Stay on the waste side of the line when cutting the plywood. Then slowly shave down to the line with a block plane and test the fit of the bottom into the drawer.

Once a snug fit is achieved, before gluing and nailing the bottom in place, double-check to make sure the drawer has remained square by running a tape measure diagonally across the drawer from corner to corner, checking in both directions. The measurements should be the same **(Photo 12)**.

Since the drawers are made entirely of plywood, let's improve their appearance with drawer fronts of 3/4" solid oak. And adding some shoe moulding around the drawer faces will dress them up even more.

The shoe moulding is mitered at the corners. The measurements and cuts should be precise in order to achieve a nice fit for your trim. You'll cut the trim on the miter saw, but measure your trim directly from the drawer front rather than by using a tape measure to ensure accuracy.

Turn the miter saw to 45° and cut one end of the shoe moulding. Place the mitered tip to the corner edge of the drawer front **(Photo 13)**. Then at the opposite end mark the backside of the moulding with a pencil. Turn the miter

saw to the opposite 45° angle and make the cut. Continue the procedure for all four pieces all the way around each drawer front.

This trim is a nice decorative touch and thereby your eye goes directly to this drawer front. However, a nail in it would draw too much attention and the hammer head might leave an ugly mark. So glue the pieces in place, using some masking tape as a "clamp" to hold it in place while the glue dries.

Once the shoe moulding is dry on both drawer fronts, attach them to the actual drawers. Drill clearance holes through the drawer box and then screw the drawer front to the drawer box.

The drawer fronts fit flush into the bench so handles are needed. The handles should be properly centered in the drawer fronts or once again your eye will really notice the mistake.

To properly position the handles, begin by dividing the drawer front in half, vertically and horizontally. This gives you the center of the drawer front.

Then measure the distance between the holes on the

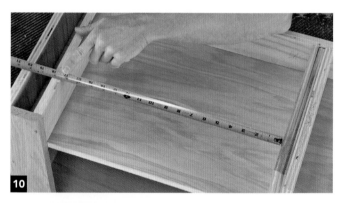

10

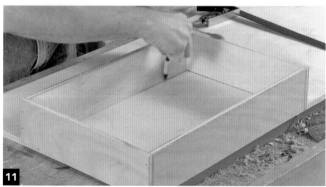

11

12

13

14

actual handle. *TIP – use a compass to set the points in the holes of the handle* **(Photo 14)**.

Then measure the spread of the compass on the tape measure. In this case, the distance was 3". So from the middle of the drawer front measure over 11/2" for the first hole, then place the compass on that pencil mark to find the spacing for the second hole **(Photo 15)**.

With the two marks established, drill the clearance holes through the drawer front and drawer, and screw the handles in place.

The drawers are done and look great, but all the raw edges of the plywood are visible. Covering these edges with oak edge banding gives all the plywood the appearance of solid oak. Edge banding is a thin veneer strip of wood that is slightly wider than the 3/4" plywood. It also has an adhesive on the back that is activated when heat is applied.

A hot iron can apply the heat to melt the glue on the back side of the banding. It's a fairly simple method however, as the glue melts the banding has the tendency to slide around. This can be frustrating. So to help minimize that, cut the edge banding to length and temporarily hold it in place with tape **(Photo 16)**. Do not place the iron on the tape. Heat the banding between the pieces of tape. Remove the iron and let the glue dry. Then peal off the tape and place the iron back on to melt the glue where the tape was.

After the glue has cooled and dried, use a razor blade and shave off the extra width of the edge banding as needed and use a sanding block to sand it flush with the plywood.

Since the top is plywood, it too receives edge banding around it. And once the banding is on, attach the top to the bench.

When placing the top on the bench, make sure to measure equal distances on both ends and front-to-back **(Photo 17)**.

The top is nailed to the bench, which doesn't give as much holding strength as a screw, so it's a good idea to add glue before nailing to give it extra holding power.

At this point the bench is built and is ready for finishing, but before applying stain give all surfaces a good sanding.

Sand the project beginning with #100-grit sandpaper. Normally I begin with #80 or sometimes #60-grit, but because the majority of this project is plywood the veneer is very thin #80- or #60-grit can easily sand right though the nice oak veneer layer and expose the plywood underneath.

In this case, begin with #100, then #150, and finish up with #220-grit. Even with the finer grit sandpaper you still need to be careful not to sand through the veneer, especially at the edges. Make sure to wipe off all dust in between each sanding of different sandpaper grits. This will help achieve a smooth finish ready for stain.

I used an oil based penetrating stain on this bench. Use a rag and work the stain into the grain of the wood with a circular motion, then wipe off excess stain with another clean rag. *NOTE – Properly dispose of oily rags so they don't spontaneously combust. Either place them in an airtight metal container or hang them outside to completely dry before disposal.*

For the topcoat, I used an oil-based polyurethane. Water-based poly dries fast, but on a larger project I prefer oil because it gives me a longer working time to achieve a smooth finish. Speaking of a smooth finish, I prefer a foam brush for the top because it doesn't leave any fiber marks from a bristle brush. But the bristle brush is good to use to fit into the corners of the trim around the drawers **(Photo 18)**.

Once your hallway bench is completed, you just might like it so much you won't let the kids sit on it to change their shoes.

Parts list in inches

QTY.	PART	THICKNESS	WIDTH	LENGTH
4	legs	$3/4$	$3^1/2$	18
2	end panels	$3/4$	14	18
2	shelves	$3/4$	14	42
1	top	$3/4$	17	48
1	back rail	$3/4$	$3^1/2$	$38^7/16$
3	short rails	$3/4$	$3^1/2$	$13^1/4$
4	drawer F & B	$1/2$	3	$17^1/8$
4	drawer sides	$1/2$	3	12
2	drawer bottom	$1/4$	$11^1/2$	$17^5/8$
2	drawer faces	$3/4$	$3^1/2$	18
1	shoe mould	$7/16$	$3/4$	96

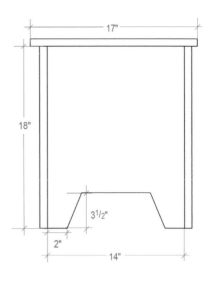

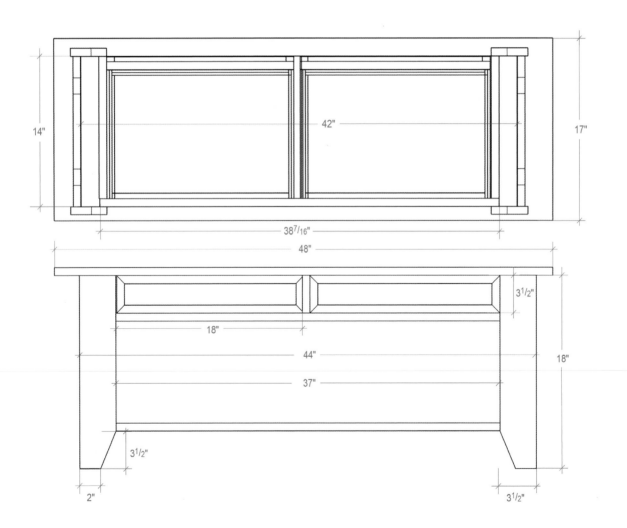

Pine Bench

A bench is a perfect seating project for the front porch, mudroom or even a three-season room. Being made out of pine, this one is fairly lightweight, yet sturdy enough to comfortably hold two people. This bench has the rear legs slightly angled to provide a more comfortable back and also greater stability for the stance. To make the bench more attractive, it has curved arms and back rail, while the seat rails are notched giving it a lighter look but maintaining the durability a good bench needs. As an extra bonus, the seat lifts up to reveal some storage space underneath. The true beauty of this bench is the fact that it's easy and fun to make.

NOTE – If the bench is intended for outdoor use, make sure to use exterior-grade screws and a water-resistant or waterproof glue for the building process. You might also consider swapping Western red cedar for the pine, as cedar is naturally weather- and insect-resistant.

We'll start by cutting the sides for the seat rails on the miter saw. To accommodate the angled shape of the bench, the backs of these rails are cut at 8° **(Photo 1)**.

Cut the 8° first on one of the ends of the side rails, then from the tip of the 8° cut, measure over 16". Adjust the blade back to zero, and then make a straight cut.

TIP – To make sure the left- and right-side seat rails are the same length, stack them on top of each other, make sure the 8° ends are flush, and then cut both pieces at the same time on the miter saw.

Now cut the front and back seat rails to length on the miter saw. Before assembling all the rails, cut decorative notches in them taken from the measurements in the plans. Carefully cut them out with a jigsaw, and clean up any rough edges from the jigsaw with a block plane, rasp or sandpaper **(Photo 2)**.

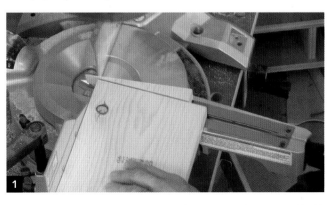

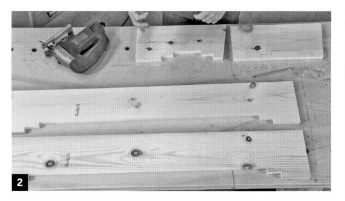

TIP – Cutting out one side of the notches allows the piece to be traced and transferred as a pattern for the others.

With all the pieces notched and cleaned up, use a pocket-hole jig to drill the side rails for assembly **(Photo 3)**. Then glue and screw the side rail pieces to the front and back rails.

Now with the seat frame made, turn your attention to the rear legs. The rear legs are made from 1x8s, but will be cut on an angle giving them the same appearance as the 1x4s used elsewhere. There are two angles on each leg, creating the lean of the back and the rake of the leg for stability.

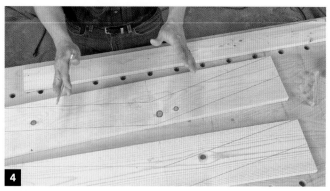

When laying out the lines make sure to mark which ends are top and bottom as there is a slight difference between the two **(Photo 4)**.

With the layout lines established on the boards, cut out the legs with a jigsaw, then smooth out the rough edges with a block plane.

When attaching the rear legs to the seat frame, placement is important. First, temporarily clamp one the of the back slats for the back rail of the seat frame. Take one back leg and align the middle point to the top edge of the seat frame on its side. Pivot the leg until the back edge of the leg is flush with the seat back slat **(Photo 5)**. Now use a pencil to trace the leg on the frame for the final position.

Drill clearance holes through the inside of the seat side rail, then glue and screw the leg in place from the inside. Repeat the process for the other rear leg.

Each front leg is made up of two pieces – a 1x4 on the side and a 1x2 for the front. This extra 1x2 for the front makes the leg look wider, but the additional thickness makes the side look too wide **(Photo 6)**. To make the side of the front leg appear the same width as the rear leg, rip 3/4" off the edge before assembly. Again use the jigsaw to rip down the 1x4, and then clean up the rough edges. Glue and nail the 1x2 to the ripped-down 1x4.

From the plans, measure up 19" from bottom of leg and make a pencil mark where the top of the seat rail will be positioned. Drill clearance holes on the seat frame and apply glue, then line up the leg with your pencil mark at the top edge of seat frame and clamp in place **(Photo 7)**. Secure the leg in place with screws driven from the back side.

With all four legs on the bench it can now sit comfortably in its upright position, and is ready for an inner stretcher between the front and back legs. This inner stretcher provides overall stability to the bench and gives it more of a nailing surface when the arm is attached. *TIP – This is a part that should not be cut ahead of time prior to this step.*

With the stretcher uncut, hold it in place and then mark the angle from the back leg onto the stretcher **(Photo 8)**. Cut the stretcher to length on the miter saw after first adjusting the blade angle of your miter saw to the pencil line.

Attach the inner stretcher to the legs with pocket screws

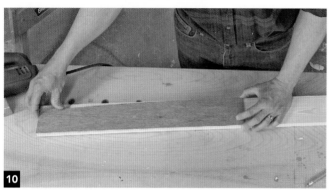

facing the outside of bench. These screws won't be visible in the finished bench, because they'll get covered up by another piece **(Photo 9)**.

The outer arm stretcher length is the distance from the front edge of the front leg to the rear edge of the back leg. Cut the outer stretcher to size, then glue and nail it to the legs and inner stretcher, neatly hiding the pocket holes and screws on the inner stretcher.

Crosscut the 1x4 for the back rail to length on the miter saw.

The bench's back rail has a slight arch across the top edge. Make a template of this arch from the plans, but you only need to make half of the arch for the template. Trace the arch from the template onto the 1x4 and flip the template to trace the other half **(Photo 10)**.

Cut the back rail out with jigsaw and smooth the arch with a block plane and then sandpaper.

The back rail is attached to the legs with pocket screws in the ends, but the workholding for this can be awkward. *TIP – Use a few spring clamps underneath the rail for the rail to rest on while screwing.*

Also the rail is not flush with the back, but sits in ¾" from back to allow room for the vertical slats. Apply glue to the ends of the rail, support it with the clamps, then pocket-screw it into place between the back legs **(Photo 11)**.

There is equal spacing between each slat and the legs. You could use a tape measure, but a compass makes fast work of setting this up. From the plans, set the compass to the width of one slat plus the spacing gap. Then mark off equal measurements across the rear bottom seat rail **(Photo 12)**.

Drill four clearance holes in the back slats, two each at top and bottom. Place a slat on the line and the corner of the slat

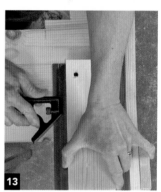

should touch the compass pencil mark. Put one screw through the slat and check for square between the rear lower seat rail and the slat **(Photo 13)**, then drive the remaining screws into the lower seat rail and upper back rail.

Repeat the same procedure for the remaining slats.

Attach some ¾" square stock around the inside bottom edge of the seat rails to support the bottom section of the storage compartment under the seat. Drill a few clearance holes in the square stock, apply glue and then screw it the rails **(Photo 14)**.

Like the seat – which we'll do shortly – the storage compartment bottom is a wide workpiece made by edge-gluing a 1x8 and 1x12 together. Sometimes when clamping up boards the glue can cause the boards to shift. So it's a good practice to leave the boards a little long during the glue up and then cut to final length after the glue has dried.

Once joined, these two boards are a little too wide to fit inside the bench. So measure the inside distance and rip the bottom to size with the jigsaw.

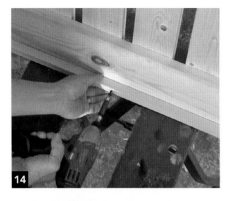

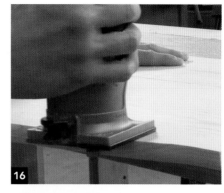

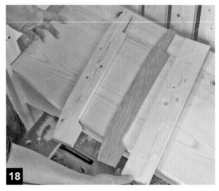

Because the back of the bench is angled, this has to be taken into account for the bottom piece. With a block plane, plane the back lower edge of the bottom piece to match the back angle. This doesn't have to be an exact fit; just enough for the bottom to fit in **(Photo 15)**. The bottom doesn't need to be nailed or screwed in place, as it can just rest on the 3/4" square stock.

Now, glue up another 1x8 and 1x12 for the seat and allow to dry.

The seat's front edge has a curved profile to it. Again, make a template from the plans and trace it onto the seat board, then cut the shape out with the jigsaw. Plane or sand away any rough edges left behind from the jigsaw.

Although the seat now has a nice curve in the front it still has a square edge. This edge can be uncomfortable on the back of your legs when sitting, but you can ease this edge and make it more comfortable by rounding it.

Use a router and a 3/8"-radius roundover bit to slightly round the top of that front edge **(Photo 16)**. Then, flip the seat over and rout the bottom of the front edge the same way. The two passes with the router neatly rounds the front in a shape called a "bullnose" edge.

To attach the seat, first set it in the bench in the open position. Mount a piano hinge to the rear edge of the seat and to the inside of the back rail. Drill pilot holes (be careful not to drill all the way through), then drive in the screws **(Photo 17)**. *TIP – Set only three screws in top and bottom for testing.*

Test closing and opening the seat. If it sticks or binds, either readjust the seat by moving the screw placements or sand any areas of the seat where it might be rubbing on the arms.

The bench arms are also taken from the plans and once again, a template is made to trace the pattern onto a 1x4. Cut out the pattern with a jigsaw, then smooth the edge with a file, rasp or sandpaper **(Photo 18)**.

Before gluing and nailing the arms to the stretchers, make sure they don't interfere with the seat opening and closing **(Photo 19)**. Once the position of the arms is good, glue and nail them on.

The bench is ready for sanding and for some color. On this project I used a golden-pine gel stain and three coats of oil-based polyurethane.

Oil-based poly takes longer to dry than a water-based poly, but it is a stronger finish. A good finishing tip is to thin the first coat of finish to a 50/50 mixture of poly and mineral spirits. This lets the poly soak in deeply, and will dry quicker. When dry, lightly sand with #220-grit sandpaper and apply a second coat that is a 75/25 mixture of poly to mineral spirits. Again, when dry, lightly sand and apply the a third coat of 100-percent poly.

If this bench is going to be used outside, use an exterior stain and an exterior finish. Exterior finishes stand up to adverse weather conditions, and contain ultraviolet blockers that protect the wood from fading or graying.

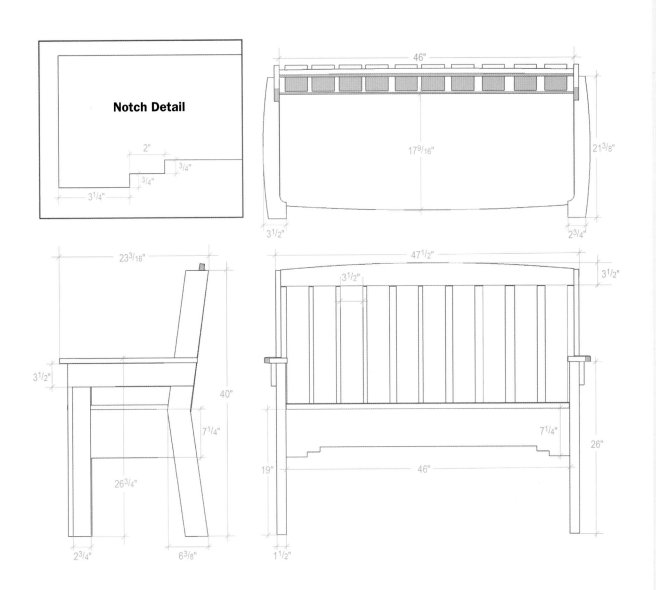

Notch Detail

Parts list in inches

QTY.	PART	THICKNESS	WIDTH	LENGTH	NOTES
2	sides	$3/4$	$7^1/4$	$15^7/16$	5° angle on back
2	front & back	$3/4$	$7^1/4$	46	
2	back legs	$3/4$	$7^1/4$	40	
2	front legs (side)	$3/4$	$2^3/4$	26	
2	front legs	$3/4$	$1^1/2$	26	
2	upper sides	$3/4$	$3^1/2$	$13^1/2$	cut to fit
2	outer sides	$3/4$	$3^1/2$	20	5° angle on back
1	back rail	$3/4$	$3^1/2$	46	top radius
10	back slats	$3/4$	$3^1/2$	24	
2	arms	$3/4$	$3^1/2$	$21^3/8$	cut to pattern
1	seat	$3/4$	$17^3/4$	$44^1/2$	cut to fit
1	bottom	$3/4$	$14^1/2$	$44^1/2$	cut to fit

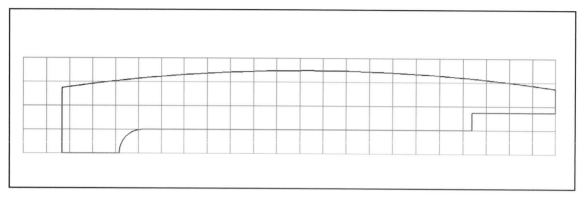

Arm Pattern: 1 square = 1"

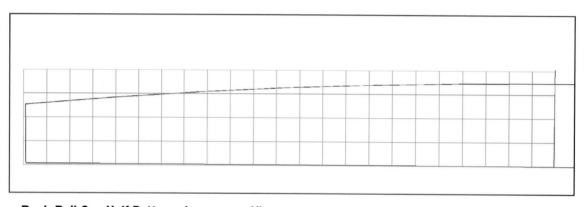

Back Rail One-Half Pattern: 1 square = 1"

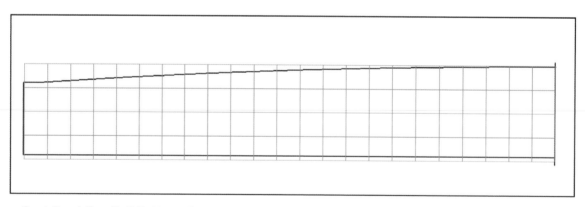

Seat Front One-Half Pattern: 1 square = 1"

Chair Steps

Chairs are among the most overworked and abused pieces of furniture in the house. We sit in them, drag them, push them and even stand on them. Go on, admit it: Even though chairs weren't meant to be stood on, we're all guilty of it. But here is a chair that's made to take it because it's designed for both sitting and standing.

At first glance it looks like any other chair in a household, but pull out the locking pin and the chair folds open to become a small step stool. This is great for changing light bulbs or to help a child get something down from a high dresser.

Like all ICDT projects, this chair is made with dimensional lumber from the big box store. I chose poplar, as it has a good balance between strength and ease of workability, but any hardwood will do. Because of the weight and stresses the chair will need to endure, I'd avoid softwood for this project.

Construction is pretty straightforward, however, this project requires precise measurements and accurate cuts for the folding action to operate properly. With that in mind, it's a great project for improving and advancing your woodworking skills.

The seat is made up of two pieces of 1x10 that are edge-glued together. Do this glue-up first so it has plenty of time to dry – you'll need it later in the project. Cut the boards

to length as noted in the cut list and place the two edges against each other. Check to see if there are any gaps. If so, plane the boards until there is a flat edge on them. Then apply some glue and clamp up the assembly.

While the seat is drying, move on to the front legs and rear upright pieces. These are made from 1x4 material. Because the legs and upright pieces have curves to them that have to be indentical on both sides, it is best to make a template on some ¼" plywood first. Use the plans to carefully draw the shape of the template, then cut it out.

Positioning of the template is important. Trace around the template onto the 1x4 so the pattern covers the full width of the 1x4. This is good because it captures the greatest amount of the straight grain in the wood, making the workpiece stronger **(Photo 1)**.

The bottom angle for the rear upright pieces is 37°, which will allow the chair to set perfectly flat on the floor. *TIP – Cut both rear legs at the same time in the miter saw* **(Photo 2)**.

Cut out the legs and rear vertical pieces using a jigsaw,

1

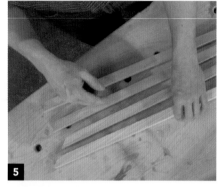

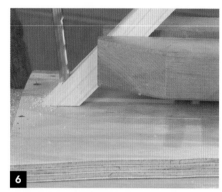

then smooth all rough edges **(Photo 3)**.

The angled rear leg is made up of two pieces that, when in the chair position, form a leg. When the chair is opened to the step stool position, it acts as a small hand rail.

The workpieces are mirrored images of each other with matching 45° angles at both ends **(Photo 4)**.

These rear angled legs are ³/₄" thick x 1" wide. You won't find this size lumber on the shelf at the big box store, so you'll need to rip it down from a wider piece. Access to a table saw would be ideal here, but you can rip it down with a jigsaw. Make sure to cut on the waste side of the line then clean up the cut by planing precisely to the line to assure both pieces are the exact same size.

Four pieces make up the two rear angled legs. Cut a 45° angle at both ends. It's important that each piece is exactly the same length **(Photo 5)**.

To get precise cuts, make the first piece at the proper length. Then, to get the remaining three pieces the exact same length, use the first one to position an auxiliary fence with a stop block and clamp it to the miter saw. *NOTE – When using a stop block the workpiece is, in effect, trapped between the blade and the stop block. Make sure to wait until the blade stops spinning before raising the blade or removing the workpiece.*

Next, prepare the rear angled legs for attachment to the front legs with glue and screws. Begin by clamping the angled leg piece with a scrap piece of wood underneath it to prevent drilling into the benchtop. You'll need to drill both a clearance hole and countersunk here. *TIP – I like to use a pocket-hole drill bit because it does both at the same time.* **(Photo 6)**.

After drilling the holes, clamp the angled rear leg piece and the front leg flat to the bench. Then attach the two pieces together with glue and a pocket screw. **(Photo 7)**.

Next are the stretchers connecting the front legs and the rear angled ones. The stretchers require accurate cuts for the length and the 45° angle, and are attached to the front legs with pocket holes and screws. *NOTE – Make sure the pocket holes face the inside of the chair so they aren't as*

noticeable when completed **(Photo 8)**.

To attach a stretcher to the rear angled leg, drill a clearance- and countersunk-hole with the pocket hole drill bit, and then fasten it with a screw.

With the front of the leg unit done, attach the other half of the angled rear leg to the upright piece **(Photo 9)**. The placement of these two pieces is important for the chair to open up properly for becoming the step stool. Take careful note of the measurements on the cut list.

Just like before, drill clearance- and countersunk-holes in the angled rear leg pieces **(Photo 10)**. Then glue and screw them to the uprights.

The left and right front leg units are joined by two rails. The upper one is placed where the seat is attached while the lower one supports what will be a step. These rails are fastened by pocket holes and screws **(Photo 11)**.

Once the rails are in place on one side unit, stand it up and clamp the other side to the rails. Check to make sure all four legs make contact with the benchtop and sit flat without any wobbling. Then screw the rails to the other side leg unit **(Photo 12)**.

With the front leg section assembled, we'll add stretchers and rails to join the two rears section together. Start by clamping the angled rear legs to the front angled leg.

Place one edge of a framing square against the front leg and draw a line where the horizontal part of the framing square crosses the rear upright of the chair **(Photo 13)**. This will be the placement for the rear rail and side stretchers.

The rear rail is pocket-holed and screwed to each upright. Use a clamp to make sure the rail doesn't move off the line then glue and screw it together **(Photo 14)**.

The side stretchers are next. The end toward the back is

a straight 90° cut. The end at the front is cut at 45°. Drill countersunk holes and clearance holes. Then with some glue, screw it to the upright and angled rear leg **(Photo 15)**.

At this point, the frame of the chair is complete and ready for the seat. To fit properly around the upright rear workpieces, the seat has to be notched at the rear corners. Center the seat on the chair frame and mark the back edge where it touches the two uprights. Then, using a combination square, measure the distance from the back rail to the edge of the seat **(Photo 16)**.

If the rear uprights were at 90° to the seat, you could easily notch and cut it out to fit. However, these uprights are on an angle, so use a bevel gauge to find the cutting angle for the notches. Place the bevel's stock flat on the stretcher and set the blade to the angle of the rear upright **(Photo 17)**.

Use the measurement from the combination square and mark the side of the seat **(Photo 18)**. Then place the bevel gauge on that mark, and draw the angle with a pencil. On the top of the seat, transfer the bevel line across

to mark the material to be cut out. Normally, you would use a jig saw to cut and notch the seat. But with the bevel angle, a hand saw is more appropriate.

The seat is cut to allow the hinge to be placed on it. With the back notches cut out, place the seat on the chair frame. On the bottom of the seat, mark where the two angled legs come together **(Photo 19)**. This is where the hinge will go.

Remove the seat and use a framing square to draw a line across the seat. Some material has to be cut off the front of the seat as well because it is too deep. And while all this cutting is being done on the seat, round off the corners to soften the edges. This will allow the hinge to function without binding or rubbing.

Once the seat is cut, use a block plane to remove any saw marks and also make a chamfer on the topside edge. That chamfer allows for the hinge barrel to set down into the seat **(Photo 20)**.

To set the hinge in place, put the seat in the vise. Use spring clamps to hold the two halves of the seat together with the chamfers facing each other. Place the piano hinge across it with the barrel splitting right down between the two halves.

Place a couple of screws in each side and test the operation of the seat **(Photo 21)**. If it moves smoothly and has proper alignment, then drive the rest of the screws into the hinge to attach it securely.

Place the seat back on the chair frame and drill clearance holes up through the rails and stretchers, then screw the seat to the frame.

Place the stock of a square flat against the front leg with the square's blade resting on the lower stretchers. Then draw a line on the rear angled legs. This will give the placement of the lower shelf so it's level and flat **(Photo 22)**.

Drill pilot holes up from the bottom through the front lower rail and attach the step/shelf with screws. On the front of the rear angled leg, drill a countersunk hole into the step/shelf, and secure it with a 2½" screw **(Photo 23)**.

Attach a lower back rail behind the shelf. Keep it flush with the top of the shelf. Trace around the rail with a pencil onto the rear upright.

The lower rear rail is pocket-screwed into place. To get access to the holes, the chair must be opened up to the step stool position. This way the holes will be hidden from view when it is closed and used as a chair. Place a clamp to hold the rail in place and glue/screw it in position **(Photo 24)**.

Close the step stool back up into the chair position. Cut and place the back upper slats in position and trace around them onto the uprights **(Photo 25)**.

Remove the back slats and from the inside drill clearance holes through the uprights. The reason for this is the back slats are not positioned directly in the middle of the vertical uprights. Also they are slightly angled to follow the curve of the uprights. By drilling from the inside out, I can be assured when I put the screws in they will go directly into the middle of the slats for the most strength **(Photo 26)**.

From the outside of the rear upright, drill countersunk holes. Place glue on the lower slat and clamp it in position. Drill pilot holes into the slat to prevent splitting, and secure with screws. Repeat for the upper slat **(Photo 27)**.

With both back slats attached, let's hide the holes and screws. The countersunk holes were made with a 3/8" drill bit, so some short sections of 3/8" dowel, glue, and a flush-cutting saw will create plugs that cover everything up nicely **(Photo 28)**.

The final step is to add a locking pin through the rear lower rail and into the shelf. The pin is necessary – without it, whenever the chair is picked up to be moved, it would unfold into the step stool position. The pin locks it all together **(Photo 29)**.

Make sure the 3/8" hole goes through the rail and into the center of the shelf **(Photo 30)**.

Any 3/8" dowel rod will work as a pin. But for a more decorative look I used a Shaker-style peg and filed it down with a rasp to fit the 3/8" size hole **(Photo 31)**.

With the pin installed, moving the chair is no problem at all.

After thoroughly sanding the chair, it's time for the stain and finish. This project was made out of poplar, which can range in color from creamy white to brown, and may even have shades of green or pink. For that reason, I chose to use a gel stain. The gel stain is thicker than penetrating stain, and mostly sits on the surface of the wood. This allows a more even coverage and more consistent color tone to help reduce the extreme color differences in the underlying wood. As a topcoat, I used a spray polyurethane that gave good coverage for the flat surfaces and also allowed me to get into the tight corners of the legs and stretchers.

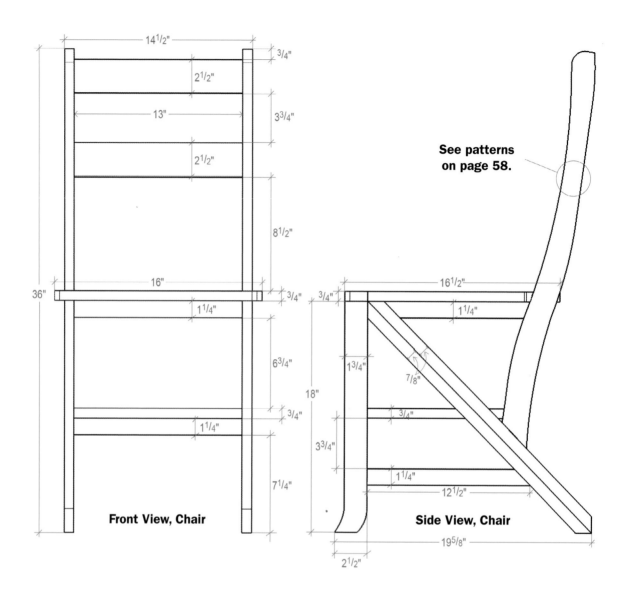

Front View, Chair

See patterns on page 58.

Side View, Chair

Parts list in inches

QTY.	PART	THICKNESS	WIDTH	LENGTH
2	straight legs	3/4	1 1/2	18
4	angled legs	3/4	7/8	25*
2	back sides	3/4	4*	30
2	back slats	3/4	2 1/2	13
4	lower rungs (front/back)	3/4	1 1/4	13
2	side rungs	3/4	1 1/4	13 1/4*
2	side rungs	3/4	1 1/4	12 1/2*
1	seat	3/4	14 3/4	16*
1	seat front	3/4	1 3/4	16*
1	shelf/step	3/4	12 1/8	13
1	hinge*			

*cut to fit

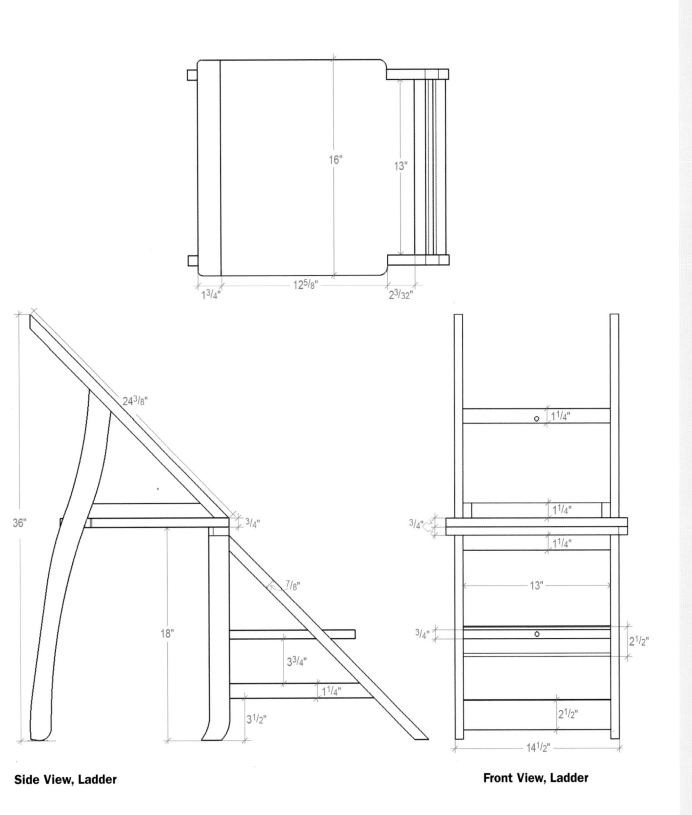

Side View, Ladder

Front View, Ladder

1 square = 1"

1 square = 1/2"

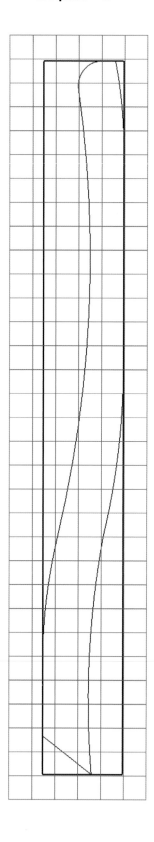

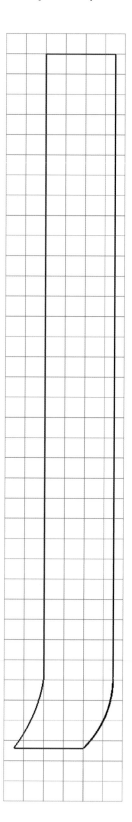

Rocking Chair

There's something about a rocking chair that makes you immediately think comfort. Sitting down to rest with a gentle back-and-forth movement certainly is relaxing, but building a rocking chair can be complicated. I wanted to build an ICDT version of a rocker using basic tools and dimensional material. After four prototypes and research into traditional Shaker style chairs, I believe I have designed a comfortable, lightweight, yet strong chair that is easy to build.

The bulk of the chair is made from 2x4s, 1-by material and some dowels. The rockers on the chair provide smooth moving action, yet have an anti-tip feature at the tail end. The back legs up to the seat are slightly shorter than the front legs. This helps make the chair lean back a little. The front legs widen out making it easy to get in and out of. The rear legs, beginning at the seat, angle slightly back. The spindles in the back bow and flex, acting as a spring or cushion for your back. All these small details make for a relaxing chair.

Begin by gluing up the seat. Make sure the two boards join without any gaps. If gaps are there, use a block plane to shave the edges until a good joint is achieved.

When gluing your boards together, tighten the clamps just enough so some glue squeezes out evenly along the joined edge. Be careful to not to over tighten the clamps. This can cause the boards to bruise or even bow the board to the point the seat is no longer flat.

With the seat drying in the clamps, start working on the legs. The legs are made out of 2x4s. Both sets of legs are angled for comfort and ease getting in and out of the chair. Cut the legs to length and lay out the cut lines to create the angles. It's a good idea to mark the area that will be waste so you don't confuse it with the area that will be kept (**Photo 1**).

NOTE – 2x4s usually have lots of knots in them. Take time to look for boards with fewer knots and review the layout to avoid a

knot at where an angle will be on the legs. Knots are weak areas and could cause the leg to break if located on the angled section.

Cut out the legs with a jigsaw, cutting on the waste side of the line (**Photo 2**). Once the legs are cut out, clean them up with a block plane and sandpaper.

Each leg has two notches and some holes. The notches support the seat rails and the rockers. The holes hold the 3/4" dowel stretchers. Take time to measure and lay out the areas that are notched and drilled – according to the plans

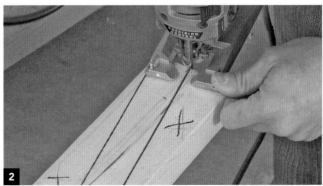

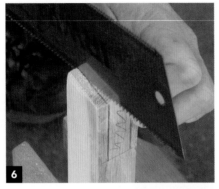

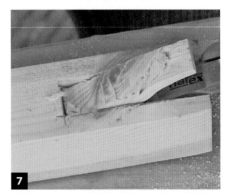

– keeping in mind that there are right and left sides to the legs **(Photo 3)**.

The rails under the seat hold the entire weight of a person. To ensure they are strong, the rails are housed inside the leg notches. Use a hand saw to carefully cut the waste area out **(Photo 4)**.

Make two crosscuts at each end of the notch area. Then turn the leg on its side and use a chisel to remove the rest of the waste **(Photo 5)**. Because the grain of the wood runs lengthwise along the leg, the area should chisel out fairly easily, but some final clean up might be necessary to properly fit the rail. It's better to cut a little small and widen the notch to fit than make your cut too large and end up with a sloppy fit for the rail fit.

The legs are also notched at the bottom where the rockers fit in between them. These notches are going to be rip cuts. Start sawing on the corner and on the inside (waste area) of the line. Saw at about a 45° angle and work the saw down to the bottom of the line **(Photo 6)**. Then turn the leg around and saw at the same 45° angle to the bottom of the line. Essentially, you've sawn a "V" on the leg. Now, hold the saw horizontal and cut again from the top all the way down to the bottom of the line, removing all the uncut material in the middle. With this side of the notch done, repeat the process for the other side.

To remove the waste, make a series of strikes with the chisel. Removing this waste will be harder here than the notch for the seat rail because the chisel is cutting across the grain.

Place the chisel on the line at the base of the notch. Strike the chisel severing the wood fibers. Then place the chisel at the end grain of the leg and strike the chisel, removing a

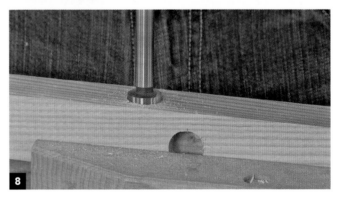

large portion of the waste **(Photo 7)**. Repeat this process to about the middle of the leg, then turn it over and do it again from the opposite side.

The notch should be 3/4" wide and 2½" deep. With a scrap piece of 1-by, test the fit of the notch. If needed, use a rasp to clean up the inside of the notch walls to make a snug fit. *NOTE – Do not use excessive force to test the fit. The leg can easily split apart and the leg will be completely ruined.*

After each notch is fitted, drill the holes for the stretchers. The stretchers are 3/4" dowels and fit into holes precisely 3/4" deep **(Photo 8)**.

TIP – To get an accurate measurement for depth, use either a dowel marked at 3/4" to test the hole depth as you drill, or wrap some tape 3/4" from the end of a drill bit. As the tape touches the wood, it will sweep away the wood chips and then it will be easy to see the depth has been achieved.

Now make the rails to fit into the legs. The rails are 1x4s ripped down to 2½". When ripping the boards to size, cut them a little wide. Then with a block plane slowly sneak up

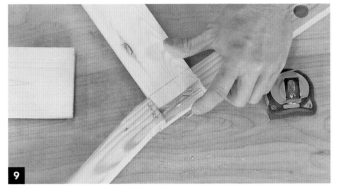

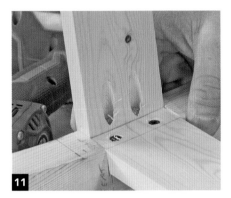

on the line, testing the fit in the notches for a good snug fit.

The rails seat into the leg notches only 3/4" deep to accommodate the rails from the other direction **(Photo 9)**. Mark 3/4" on the rail and line the pencil mark up with the edge of the leg.

Drill clearance holes through the rails, going on a slight angle. This is to help the screw go into the middle of the leg and not out on the edge where it would be weaker. Cut the dowel stretchers to the same length as the rail. With glue on the dowel and glue and screws on the rail, attach them to the legs **(Photo 10)**. It's a good idea to put a clamp across the dowel stretcher while the glue is drying.

The front section is done. Repeat the same procedure for the back legs.

The rails connecting the sides to the back are also screwed to the legs. For these, use pocket holes and screws with the holes placed on the inside, hiding them from view **(Photo 11)**.

Apply glue to the ends of both side rails, and fit them into the notches on the front section. Because pocket screws have the tendency to slightly move when tightened down, first clamp the rails in snuggly, then use the screws to fasten them together.

Glue and place the side dowel stretchers in place, and then attach the front section to the back section. Again, use a clamp to prevent the rails from moving out of the notches and screw it into place **(Photo 12)**.

With the chair in clamps and drying, make the upper back rail. Cut the rail to length, then make a template from the plans and trace it onto the 1x4 rail. Cut it out with a jigsaw and smooth any rough edges **(Photo 13)**.

Rather than leave the top arc of the upper rail square and sharp, softening it by rounding it over would be a nice touch. You can use a rasp and sandpaper for this, but a router and a roundover bit does a quicker job.

The lower rear rail is also from a 1x4, but rip it down to 2" with the jigsaw **(Photo 14)**.

The spindles making up the chair's back are actually 1/2" dowels. The dowels will bow and flex quite a bit, acting like a cushion for one's back. The spacing of the dowels is so they ride along both sides of your spine, making it quite comfortable. These dowels are set into the upper and lower rails.

From the plans, mark out the spacing on the lower rail for the 1/2" dowels and drill 3/4" deep on each mark. Again, use the trick of a scrap piece of dowel marked off at 3/4" (or tape wrapped at 3/4" around your drill bit) to make sure the depth is correct. Repeat the same procedure for the upper rail **(Photo 15)**.

The upper rail fits at the top between the two rear legs. Drill 3/8" countersunk holes, as well as clearance and pilot

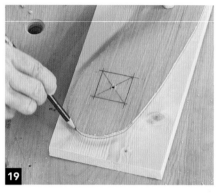

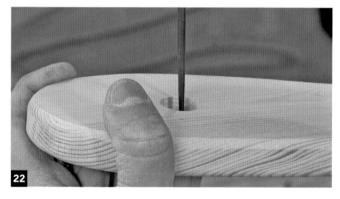

holes through the outside face of the legs into the end of the rail. Then, apply glue to the ends of the rail and drive in some 2¹/2" screws to hold the rail in place.

The legs slightly angle back, so it's important to have the rail on the same angle. Set a combination square to the distance the rail should set back and make sure the rail is running parallel to the legs. (Photo 16).

The lower rail is also set back the same distance and attached the same way, however there is a problem. The lower rail is on the part of the leg where the leg is straight, but it should be at the same angle as the upper rail so the dowel holes are in line with each other. To do this, drill and drive one screw on each side of the rail to temporarily attach it to the legs. Then place a straightedge so it is resting on the top and lower rail at the same time (Photo 17).

Then twist the lower rail so it pivots and the yardstick is flat on the face of the rail (Photo 18). Now the upper and lower are in perfect alignment with each other. Drill and drive the remaining screws into the lower rail.

Once the lower rail is in the correct position, measure the distance between the two rails for the dowel spindles. But remember that each spindle goes into a ³/4" hole, so add another 1¹/2" to get the correct length of the dowels.

Cut the spindles to the proper length. Now, remove the lower rail, place the spindles into the holes on the rails, and attach the lower rail permanently.

From the plans, make a template for the arm shape and trace it onto a piece of 1-by material (Photo 19). With the jigsaw, cut out each arm and smooth the edges with a rasp and sandpaper.

Just like with the upper rail, the edges on the chair arms should be slightly rounded over for comfort. Use the router with a roundover bit (Photo 20).

The armrest pattern has a reference mark on it where a screw attaches the arms to the front legs. Begin by drill a ³/4" countersunk hole and then a clearance hole for the screw (Photo 21).

Place the arm into position in the chair, keeping the back

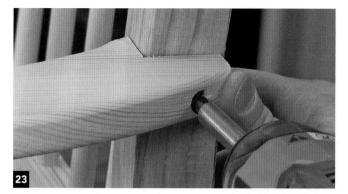

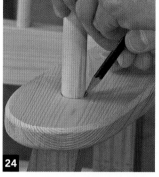

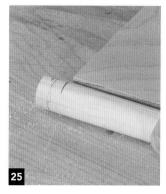

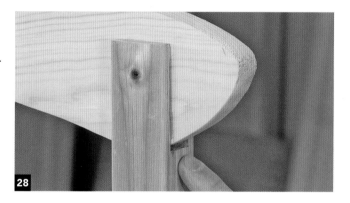

of the arm tight against the rear leg. Then place an awl into the clearance hole and make a mark on the top of front leg **(Photo 22)**. In theory, the mark should be in the center of the front leg. But mismeasuring of the arm, drilling the hole, the rail, warping of the legs, or a combination of all four, can result in the mark being slightly off from center. It won't matter much. Drill a hole on the awl mark and secure the arm with a screw.

Once the front of the arm is attached to the front leg, drill a 3/8" countersunk hole and clearance hole through the rear side of the armrest. Follow this up with a pilot hole into the rear leg, and then fasten it into place with a screw **(Photo 23)**.

As we've done in earlier projects, plug the holes with a 3/8" dowel. Apply some glue to the end of the dowel, twist it into the hole and then cut it off flush **(Photo 24)**.

The hole in front of the arm is plugged with a 3/4" dowel. I could place the 3/4" dowel rod in it and cut it flush like the others. But as a little decorative feature I wanted it to stand proud. Something fun for your hands to feel when sitting in the chair.

Begin by placing the dowel in and with a pencil mark the depth of the hole around the dowel. Remove the dowel and make two other measurements. From the end of the dowel measure down 1/4" and make a mark. This will be the amount that will stick above the arm when it's finally put into place.

From the depth pencil line, measure down another 1/4". This is where the dowel rod will actually be cut off **(Photo 25)**. Soften the square end of the dowel with a rasp, filing over the edges to that pencil mark **(Photo 26)**. When you have it nicely rounded, clean it up with sandpaper. Cut the dowel at the third mark. Add some glue to the bottom and tap it into place in the armrest.

The rockers are next. You could cut them out of a 1x6, but it's pretty tight and it is very possible to have a flat spot on the rocker. So a 1x8 would be better because good smooth rocking is essential for a nice rocking chair. A wider board means there is more material to shave off if necessary to achieve a smooth graceful arc. Again, make a template and cut out the rockers with a jigsaw. Smooth the rough edges and test each rocker on the workbench, making sure there are no flat areas on it **(Photo 27)**.

Test the fit in the notches at the bottoms of the legs. The fit should be snug, but not tight **(Photo 28)**. If it feels like you're applying too much pressure, stop. Forcing the rocker into place will split the leg. If need be, use a rasp and remove some material in the inside making it easier to slide the rocker into place.

Once you've achieved a decent fit, each rocker must be

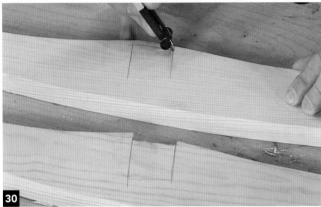

positioned in the same place for a smooth gliding action to perform. From the tip of the front of the rocker, measure back 2". This is where the rocker will sit in the notches of the front leg.

Once the rockers are in place, for the most part it's good to go. However, because the rockers are curved and the notches are cut straight at the base there is a small gap. At the back side of the notch the rocker makes full contact, but the curve reveals a gap on the front side of the notch. To hide these gaps, use a compass and set the compass to the size of the gap **(Photo 29)**.

Remove the rocker and with that setting on the compass, trace it on the rocker. The gap on the front will be different than the rear so repeat this step for each leg. Then cut out the material to be removed **(Photo 30)**.

Cutting out the notches is easily done with a saw cutting down the lines. And because the grain is running the with the board, a strike with a chisel will easily knock out the waste material, just like with the notch for the seat rail on the legs earlier.

Notching the rockers gives it a nice clean look once they're placed back in the legs **(Photo 31)**.

To hold the rocker in its final resting position, drill a 3/8" hole all the way through the leg and rocker. Then glue a 3/8" dowel through it. Use a dowel slightly longer than you need, and once it's dry use a flush-cutting saw to trim both sides even with the sides of the leg.

From the plans, cut the seat to its proper width and length, then notch the corners of the seat to fit around the legs. Using a combination square, measure each leg and then cut it out a matching spot in the corners of the seat with a jigsaw. Finally, use a router and roundover bit on the front edge of the seat. This will make it more comfortable on the backs of your legs when sitting in the chair.

It's not a bad idea to cut the notches around the legs a little larger. The seat is solid wood and it will want to expand and contract through the seasons. The slightly wider notch gives it room to grow **(Photo 32)**. Also, don't glue the seat down. Instead use pocket screws on the inside of the rails. Slightly elongate the holes, giving it room to expand.

With the seat in place, give the chair a thorough sanding in preparation for stain and a final finish. I chose a gel stain for this chair. As we've noted before, pine has the tendency to "splotch" and gel stain helps minimize that. For the final clear finish, I chose spar urethane. The spar urethane is best for outdoors applications. However, I like it because it has a "yellowish" hue to it, making it look more like an antique.

This chair is ideal for just about anyone in the family. One can relax in it sipping an ice-cold lemonade, or soothing a baby back to sleep. I'm sure you'll like this chair so much that it will quickly become a member of the family.

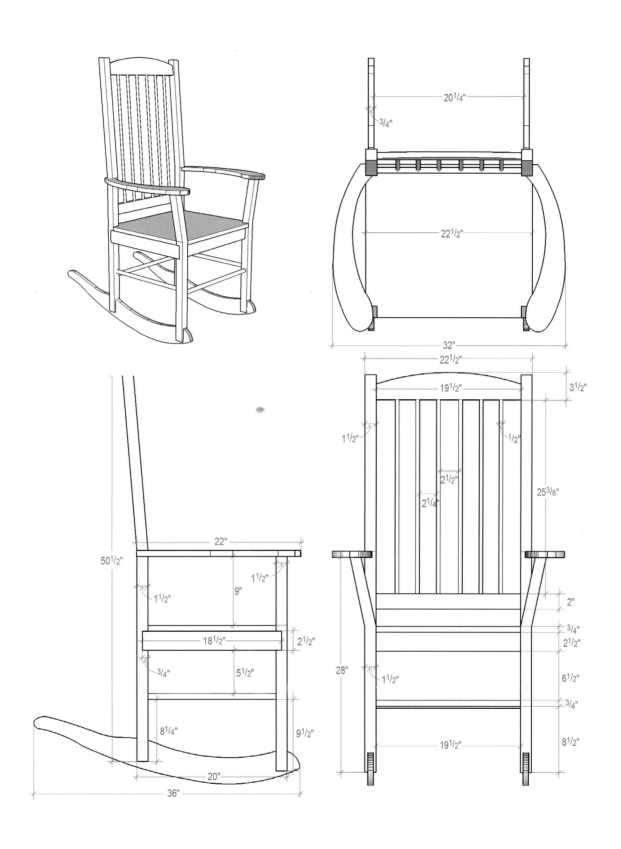

Parts list in inches

QTY.	PART	THICKNESS	WIDTH	LENGTH	NOTES
2	rear legs	$1^1/_2$	$1^1/_2$	$50^1/_2$	cut from $3^1/_2$ wide piece
2	front legs	$1^1/_2$	$1^1/_2$	28	cut from $3^1/_2$ wide piece
1	top back rail	$3/_4$	$3^1/_2$	$19^1/_2$	shape to pattern
1	lower back rail	$3/_4$	2	$19^1/_2$	
6	back spindles	$1/_2$	$1/_2$	27	cut length to fit
2	side stretchers	$3/_4$	$2^1/_2$	$18^1/_2$	
2	front & rear stretchers	$3/_4$	$2^1/_2$	$19^1/_2$	
2	side foot rails	$3/_4$	$3/_4$	$18^1/_2$	cut length to fit
2	front & rear foot rails	$3/_4$	$3/_4$	21	cut length to fit
2	rockers	$3/_4$	6	36	shape to pattern
2	arms	$3/_4$	6	20	shape to pattern
1	seat	$3/_4$	20	$22^1/_2$	notch corners

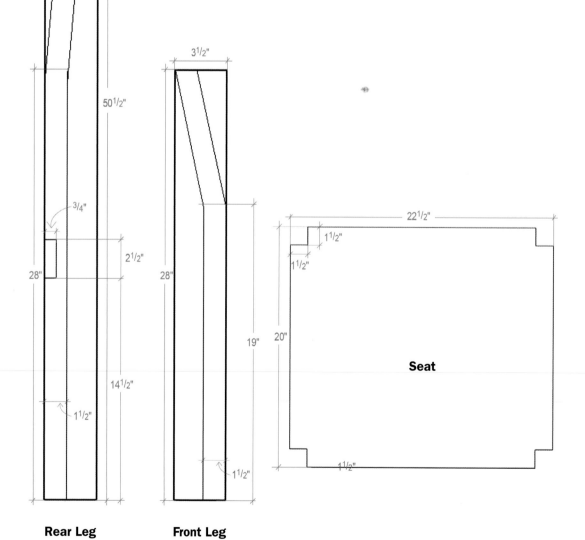

Rear Leg

Front Leg

Seat

**Rocker Pattern,
1 square = 1"**

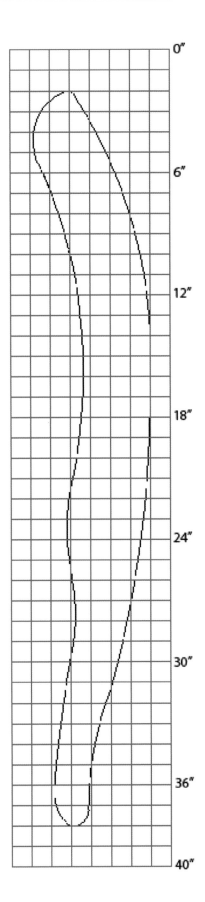

0"

6"

12"

18"

24"

30"

36"

40"

**Arm Pattern,
1 square = 1"**

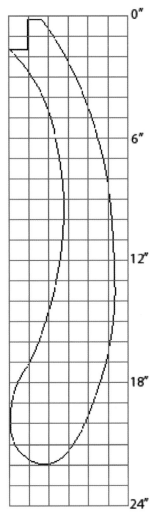

0"

6"

12"

18"

24"

Tool Chest

Every traditional workshop has a wooden tool chest. But the tool chest doesn't have to be confined to the shop. Many people will use a chest of this same design elsewhere in the house to store blankets, clothes or even toys for kids. With so many uses, this chest has virtually become a hallmark piece of furniture for any home.

You don't have to go out and purchase a mass-produced one from an outlet store. Making your own chest is an easy project requiring little more than a trip to your local big box store, three boards and a Saturday afternoon. The three boards used to make this chest are a 6'-long 1x12 and two 8'-long 1x8s.

The building process begins with the ends for the chest. Before making any cuts, check the ends of the board to make sure they are square – never assume the factory edge is square and true. Crosscut the 1x12 to length with a miter saw, or a circular saw and square **(Photo 1)**.

Mark an "X" on the waste side of the line to make sure you place the blade on the correct side to assure the board comes out to the correct length.

TIP – When measuring multiple pieces on a single board make sure to account for the thickness of the blade, otherwise the remaining pieces will come out a little short. It's better to measure and cut each piece individually.

The ends have two arches at the bottom that form the chest legs. To create the arch, first draw a horizontal line 11$1/16$" up from the bottom edge. Then from each of the ends, measure over 4$1/16$" and make a mark on the horizontal line. Place the end pieces flat on the bench with the bottom edges butted up to each other. Set a compass at 5$1/4$", then place the point of the compass on one of the marks and draw an arch on the opposite board it butts up to **(Photo 2)**.

Once all four arches are penciled in cut them out with a jigsaw **(Photo 3)**.

Use a file or sandpaper to smooth out any rough edges and marks left behind by the jigsaw.

The front and back of the chest use a total of four 1x8s. Just like before, use the miter saw or circular saw to cut the boards to the proper length.

The front and back faces are two boards butted against each other. Place two boards side by side and look for any gaps. If needed, use a block plane to smooth out the edges and recheck to make sure the gaps are gone.

Once the boards have a good joining edge to them, make a decorative chamfer on them. On one of the boards, measure $1/4$" from the edge and draw a line lengthwise on the face of the board. Then turn the board on its edge and measure $1/4$" and draw a line lengthwise on the edge grain. This is the section to remove to form the chamfer.

Place the board securely in a vise and shave down to both pencil lines with a block plane. Repeat this for all four boards **(Photo 4)**.

The front and back pieces are glued and nailed to the ends. But before attaching them, drill $1/16$" holes to prevent potentially splitting the boards when driving in the 1$1/2$", 3d nails.

Getting the first board nailed to the end can be awkward.

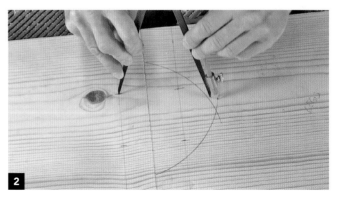

A good tip is to use a spring clamp on the end board to give it a wider base for better balance **(Photo 5)**.

Glue and nail all four boards to the ends, then use a nail set to sink the nails slightly below the surface of the board.

The chest bottom is supported by cleats running along the lower inside edge of the chest. Glue and nail ¾" square stock to the inside lower edge of the front and back pieces **(Photo 6)**.

Measure the inside of the chest and crosscut the 1x12 bottom to length. Test fit the board in the chest **(Photo 7)**. It might be a little tight; if so, use a block plane to custom-fit the bottom. If necessary, chamfer the bottom edge on one side so the piece tilts in with ease.

TIP – It's okay to have the bottom a little loose in the chest. The bottom piece is a solid piece of wood and will expand and contract with the seasons. So a little room to grow is not a bad idea.

Don't use any glue on the bottom. The glue would restrict the natural seasonal movement of the wood. However, you should drive a few nails through the sides into the end grain

of the bottom board **(Photo 8)**. The nails will be able to flex just enough to let the wood move, and still keep the bottom from falling out if the chest is turned over.

The lid is two pieces of 1x8 joined together. Because the two boards will be mated together, check for gaps. If necessary, use the block plane to eliminate the gaps and make a chamfer on the mating edges the same way you did on the sides.

The tool chest lid has an overhang on the front of edge to make it easy for fingers to grab to lift open **(Photo 9)**. However, the two 1x8s together form too much of an overhang. Use a jigsaw to rip 1" off the edge of one of the 1x8. Save this scrap; we'll use it later. Use the block plane and remove the saw marks on both pieces.

Apply some glue to the mating edges of the two 1x8 workpieces, and clamp them together to dry.

Although today's glue is very strong, the lid needs more strength to withstand the multiple openings and closings the chest will undergo. Use that scrap cutoff piece from

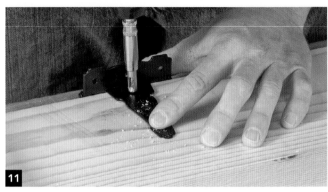

earlier to form a batten to bridge the two halves of the lid, making it more rigid and solid.

Mark the width of the lid on the scrap cutoff and cut it to length on the miter saw **(Photo 10)**. Also, ease the front ends of the battens with a 45° cut.

When attaching the batten, don't apply glue the whole length. Instead, apply only a small amount of glue near the middle and use nails to secure the batten to the lid boards. Again, because the lid is solid wood, it will want to expand and contract. The glue at the middle still allows the wood to expand in both front and back directions.

With the lid done, secure it to the chest with hinges. I used strap hinges for a decorative detail, although a variety of hinges are available at any big box store or woodworking supplier.

The tough part of any hinge is getting the screw exactly in the center of the hole. An error in drilling can cause difficulty mounting the hinge, and also affect the proper operation of the hinge. A nice tool to own is a self-centering drill bit **(Photo 11)**. A self-centering drill bit automatically finds the center of the hole on the hinge, and drills a pilot hole for the screw. NOTE – Self-centering bits come in different sizes, so be certain to buy the correct size needed for your projects.

The placement of the hinge butts up against the back edge of the lid. Drill pilot holes, then drive in the screws. Repeat the same procedure for both hinges on the lid and back of the tool chest.

Test the operation of the lid opening and closing. If minor dragging or rubbing occurs, use a file or sandpaper to ease the tight spots.

Handles are an option you can consider, and they can be attached with the same procedure as the hinges. Handles definitely help when carrying and moving the chest. However, if the chest has a permanent place in the home or shop, handles won't be necessary.

The final steps to complete this project are the stain and finish. I used pine for this project and pine is prone to "blotch" when stain is applied. "Blotching" is what happens when the wood absorbs stain at different consistencies. The result of this uneven absorption is various sections of the wood looking darker and lighter in a concentrated area. There are a few tricks to help minimize this unsightly look.

One trick is to use a gel stain, which is thicker than liquid stains. Because the gel stain is thicker, it cannot penetrate as deeply as liquid stains. Instead, the gel sits mostly on the surface of the wood and gives a more even, consistent tone.

The top coat on this tool chest is an oil-based polyurethane. Oil-based poly has a slightly yellowish/golden hue when cured due to the oil content. This hue adds to the color of the stain and gives a more "antique-ish" look to it. However, if you desire a true clear finish, then use a water-based poly. Water-based poly dries very fast, so on larger projects oil-based poly might be more desirable for more time to apply the finish evenly.

Whether you use oil- or water-based poly, lightly sand the surface with #220-grit sandpaper in between each dry coat. This knocks off any "nibs" or fine dust in the finish and also helps prepare the next coat to bind to the previous layer. Do this procedure for a minimum of three coats.

The chest is done and ready to find the perfect place in your home. It's just the right size with plenty of room for storage. And regardless of whether the chest is used in the shop to be filled with tools, or in the house filled with other household items, everyone will agree it's a welcome addition to any room in the home.

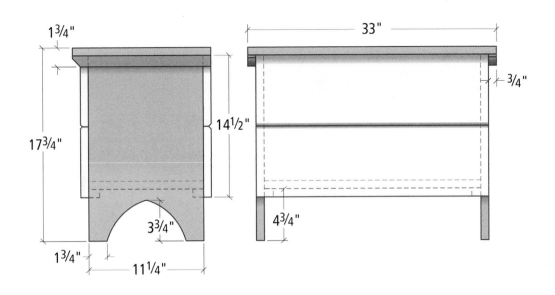

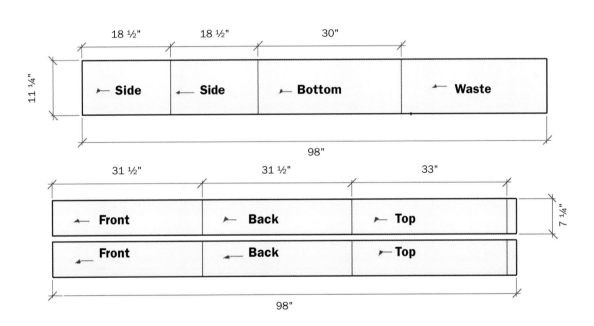

Parts list in inches

QTY.	PART	THICKNESS	WIDTH	LENGTH
4	fronts/back	3/4	7 1/4	31 1/2
2	tops	3/4	7 1/4	33
2	sides	3/4	11 1/4	18 1/2
1	bottom	3/4	11 1/4	30
2	battens	3/4	1	14 1/2
	cleats*	3/4	1	72

*cut to fit

Modern Chest on Stand

Everyone needs storage space. Whether storing tools in your shop or hiding paperwork in your office, this modern chest on a stand will look great anywhere in your home. The stand brings the chest up to a comfortable height, making for easy access to the cabinet, while the wide legs on the stand make it easier to sweep under when cleaning. Inside the cabinet are adjustable shelves to accommodate any size items to be placed in it. And the doors close nicely with three-way adjustable hinges for perfect alignment and spacing.

Make the stand first, beginning with the top. The top is made up of a 1x12 and 1x6 that you'll glue together. Cut the boards a little longer than the final measurement. Check the two edges to be glued by placing them together and look for gaps. If a gap is present, use a block plane and recheck the boards, making sure the gap is gone and the mating edges are flat and square.

Apply glue to the edges and place in clamps to dry. Proper clamping pressure is important – too much pressure can cause the boards to bow. Apply enough pressure that just a small amount of glue squeezes out. *TIP – If using pipe clamps, the glue can react to the metal pipe and create black marks on the wood surface. To avoid this, wrap some tape around the pipe where glue squeeze-out will occur.* Set the top aside to dry. Once it comes out of the clamps, crosscut the top to its final finished length.

Each leg consists of three 1x3 boards faced-glued together. A 1x3 is actually ³⁄₄" x 2¹⁄₂", so three of them together will form 2¹⁄₂" wide by 2¹⁄₄" in depth. Because these are not the same dimensions, make sure to mark and keep the wider 2¹⁄₂" sides as the fronts of the legs. This will help for proper assembly later. Cut each piece for the legs a little longer than the final dimension.

When gluing up the legs, it is important to keep them square because you'll attach stretchers to them later. Assembly will be difficult if the legs are not square. Use the same technique for gluing and clamping the legs as you used for the top (Photo 1). After all of the legs are dry and out of the clamps, double-check to make sure each leg is flat and square and use the block plane again if necessary. Use a miter saw to cut the legs to final length. A stop block on your saw assures each leg is exactly the same length.

Aprons and stretchers connect the legs together. The aprons, cut from 1x6 stock, are the pieces at the top of the legs. They'll have an arch on them, with the thinnest part of the arch 3¹⁄₂" wide. (The same width as the 1x4s you'll use shortly for the stretchers).

To make the arch, find the center of the board. Measure up 3¹⁄₂" from the edge and tap a nail at that mark. Tap a nail in near the bottom corners of the board. Now, take a thin strip of wood longer than the board, and wrap it around the nails causing the strip to bow. With a pencil, trace the arch (Photo 2). Repeat the process for the other aprons. Cut the arches out with a jigsaw and smooth up the edges with a file or sandpaper.

Begin the assembly process with what will become the sides first. This is important, because if the front and back are made first, there will be no room for the drill to attach the pocket screws for the sides. Place two legs on the bench and place the side apron with the pocket holes facing up. The apron should not be flush with the face of the legs – an offset is needed. To create the offset, place a scrap piece of 1-by stock under the face of the apron. Keep the top of the legs even with the top of the apron and drill pocket holes on the inside surface at each end of the aprons and use pocket screws to attach them to tops of the legs (Photo 3). Also, drill a few vertical pocket holes on the upper edge of the aprons to attach the top later.

NOTE – The top is made of solid wood, so elongate the holes to allow for the seasonal movement of expanding and contracting to take place.

Drilling the pocket screws leaves behind unsightly holes, but the top will conceal these holes once it's attached. This is not the case with the lower stretchers. Those pocket holes would be visible, so we'll attach the stretchers to the legs by drilling through the legs and into the stretchers behind them. We'll hide the screw heads later with wooden plugs.

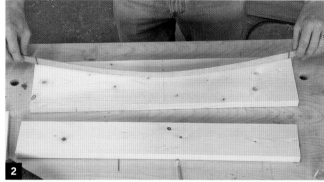

unlike the pocket screws that have self-tapping threads, the 2½" screws for the stretchers don't have that feature. So you have to drill a pilot hole first to avoid cracking and splitting the stretcher.

If the drill bit for the pilot hole is not long enough to go through the legs and into the stretcher at the same time, place the stretcher in position and stick an awl through the clearance hole to make a mark on the stretchers **(Photo 4)**. Before removing the stretcher for drilling, mark its position so you don't reinstall it in the wrong place. Drill the clearance holes then apply glue and screw into place **(Photo 5)**. Repeat the process for the other side. Attach the front and back aprons and stretchers with the same procedure **(Photo 6)**.

If it's dry, remove the top from the clamps. We didn't cut the top boards to length before glueup to allow for possible shifting of the boards, so cut the top to the measurement on the plans.

Place the top on the workbench with the underside side facing up, then upend the leg assembly and place it on the top. Measure equal distances from the sides and front to get the leg unit centered. As mentioned before, the top is attached to the leg unit by means of pocket screws in the holes you drilled earlier. Because the top must be able to move freely with seasonal changes, don't use any glue **(Photo 7)**.

The countersunk holes on the stretchers are still visible, so let's cover up the screws. Apply some glue to a ⅜" dowel and place the dowel in the hole. Use a flush-cutting saw to trim away the excess dowel. Finish by sanding the legs smooth. The stand is completed and can be set aside while you make the cabinet.

Just like the top of the stand, the top of the cabinet is glued up of two boards, put in clamps and set aside to dry.

The front and back stretchers are lower than the side stretchers. This offset will avoid the mishap of the screws intersecting with each other.

It's very important to label the legs individually to avoid any confusion when drilling for the stretchers. Before drilling, double-check the plans for the proper placement of each stretcher.

Begin by measuring and countersinking a ⅜" hole into the legs. Then change drill bits and make a clearance hole all the way through the legs – the clearance holes' diameter should be slightly larger than the diameter of the screw. When drilling, use a sacrificial board underneath to avoid drilling into the top of your bench. Do this for the placement of all the stretchers on all the legs.

 Place the stretcher in position and again use a scrap piece of 1-by under it to give it the same offset as the aprons. Drill a pilot hole before gluing and screwing the stretcher in place. (Your pilot holes' diameter should be slightly smaller than the diameter of the screw). A pilot hole is needed because

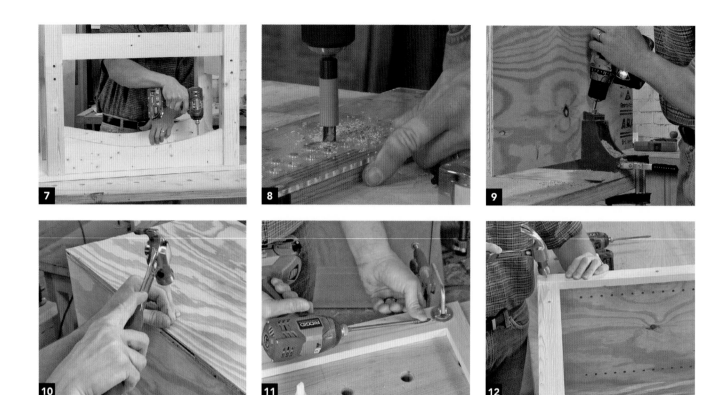

Once the top is dry and out of the clamps, cut it to final length before attaching it to the carcase.

The rest of the cabinet is mostly made of 3/4" plywood. Plywood is very stable for furniture construction and more affordable than solid wood. From the plans, use a circular saw and straightedge to cut out the sub top, bottom and side pieces for the cabinet carcase.

With the individual pieces all cut to proper size and checked for square, place the side pieces on the workbench with the insides facing upward. These sides receive a series of equally spaced holes that hold shelf pins for the adjustable shelves.

The holes must be perfectly spaced, or the shelf will be crooked and will rock. A shelf-pin jig has holes equally spaced on it and the drill bit fits into the hole on the jig to drills countersink holes at a specific depth to prevent from drilling all the way through **(Photo 8)**. Two common sizes for shelf pins are 5mm and 1/4". *TIP – Use 1/4" and the shelf pins can be cut from a 1/4" dowel.*

Once the drilling of the shelf pins holes is finished, drill pocket holes in the sub top and bottom pieces. These pocket holes will attach the back and sides together. The placement of the holes is on the back side of each of the pieces **(Photo 9)**.

Begin by gluing and screwing the bottom to the back piece. The bottom piece sit up 1 1/2" from the bottom edge of the back piece to accommodate a face frame we'll attach to it later.

Apply glue to one of the side pieces and screw the bottom to the side. Continue working around the carcase until all the pieces, sub top and sides are attached. Although the sides have screws holding them by the sub top and bottom, it's still a good

practice to drive some nails through the sides into the back before the glue dries to give it extra strength **(Photo 10)**.

The face frame measurements can be taken from the plans, but when building it's a good idea to get exact measurements from the carcase that was just built. If the carcase was built slightly longer or smaller the face frame pieces from the plans would be wrong.

The side stiles and bottom rail are standard 1x2 materials, but the upper rail is wider. This is because the rail has to be wide enough to accept the trim added later. Rip the upper rail to size with a jigsaw and then clean up the cut with a block plane.

The face frame is fastened together by placing pocket screws in the rails, and then glued and screwed to the stiles **(Photo 11)**. When complete, glue and nail the face frame onto the front of the carcase. **(Photo 12)**.

It's a good idea to put clamps on the face frame and carcase until the glue completely dries. While the cabinet is drying turn your attention to the doors.

The door stiles and rails are made from dimensional 1x3 lumber cut to the sizes on the cut list. Although you could construct the doors with pocket screws, we'll make them with dowel pins.

The dowel pins act as small mortise-and-tenon joints and won't leave any visible holes, unlike the pocket-screw method.

When using dowels for joinery, it is important to mark the pieces in a sequential order to have the door fit properly. With the rail fitting flush to the edge of the stile, draw two lines across the rail and going into the stile approximately an inch apart from each other. Also, label the joint between each rail and matching stile with either "A, B, C and D" or "1, 2, 3, and

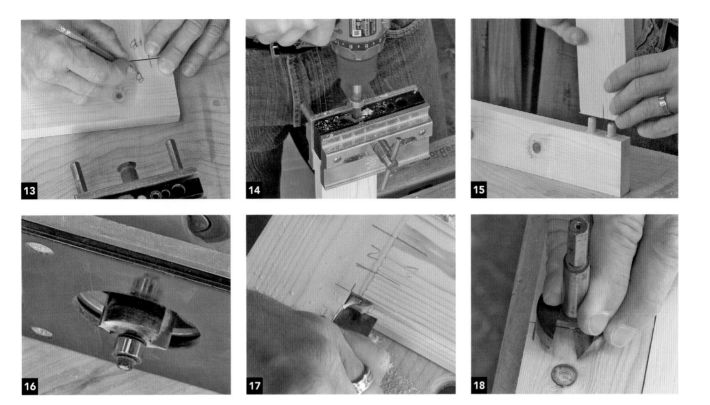

4" to keep them straight **(Photo 13)**.

There are several ways to do doweling, but money is well spent on a doweling jig to make the most accurate holes into the stiles and rails. The jig has different size holes to accept different size dowels. This project will use ³/₈" dowel pins, so align the ³/₈" mark on the jig to the pencil marks on the workpiece. Use a ³/₈" drill bit with a stop collar to prevent overdrilling the workpiece **(Photo 14)**. Follow the same procedure for all the marks on the stiles and rails.

Apply glue to the inside of the holes, on the edge of the workpiece and around the dowel pins. Dowel pins are different from regular dowels in that the edges are slightly chamfered to make starting them into the holes easier. They also have small grooves that run lengthwise to allow glue to get around it **(Photo 15)**.

Glue up and assemble the door, making sure to match up the proper stiles and rails, and place the door into some clamps. However, do not place the clamps right at the edge of the door frame. Set them in a little to allow access for a tape measure to go diagonally across the door corners to check for squareness. The measurements should both be the same going from corner to corner diagonally. If one diagonal is longer than the other, the assembly is out of square and needs to be racked. Slightly squeeze the diagonal direction that is too long to compress it slightly and check the measurements again.

Once both measurements are the same, slowly apply clamping pressure equally to both clamps at the same time. When the clamps are snug, check the measurements one more time and then set aside to dry.

Once the door frame is dry and out of the clamps, we'll fit the panel. The panel is some ¹/₄" plywood that is ¹/₂" wider and taller than the opening on the door frame. The panel could simply be glued and nailed to the inside of the door frame, but a much cleaner look is to have the panel sit inside and flush with the door frame. Use a router with a ¹/₄" rabbeting bit. This bit will make a cut ¹/₄" down and ¹/₄" into the frame **(Photo 16)**.

Before routing, clamp the door frame on the bench to prevent it from moving. A rule of thumb to remember when routing on the outside edge is to go counter-clockwise. However, this will be on the inside of the frame so it must go clockwise. When the routing is completed, use a chisel to square up the rounded corners **(Photo 17)**.

Test fit to make sure the panel fits properly. Then brush glue into the rabbet. Don't use too much because the glue can squeeze out onto the face of the panel and be visible on the outside. Set the panel in place and nail it in place with some small brad nails.

Next are the door hinges. A wide variety of hinges are available, but European style cup hinges have adjustment screws that allow you to tweak the gaps and alignment on the doors. Plus, these hinges are completely concealed once the door is closed. With any hinge, read the directions for installation. These particular hinges require a ¹/₂"-deep 35mm diameter mounting hole ¹/₈" from the edge of the stile, which you can drill with a Forstner bit **(Photo 18)**.

It's important to check and make sure the hinges sit flush in the stile. It's also important that the hinges aren't crooked or the door will bind when closing. Test fit the hinges into the holes and adjust as needed, then use the supplied screws to hold the hinges in place. To drill the holes for the hinge screws,

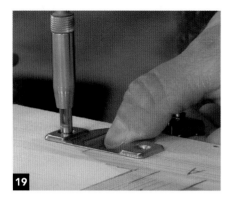

use a self-centering drill bit to place the holes exactly in the centers of the hinge openings **(Photo 19)**.

With all the hinges attached to the doors, hold off on mounting them to the cabinet. If the doors are mounted they might get in the way of attaching the top and trim, so let's do those first.

To attach the top, drill holes on the top side of the carcase, and then elongate the holes. The reason for the elongated holes is because the top is a solid piece of wood and it will want to expand and contract with seasonal changes. Place the top piece on the workbench with the bottom facing up, then set the carcase upside-down on the top. Measure equal distances from side-to-side and keep the back of the cabinet flush with the back edge of the top. Use pan-head screws to attach the carcase to the top, but don't use glue.

Cut and attach the trim while the whole unit is still upside-down. The trim is made up of two different mouldings – a profiled stop moulding and a cove moulding. Begin with the stop moulding and make a 45° cut on the end of the stock. *TIP – Shade the edge of the 45° cut with a pencil to make it easier to see when lining up with the corner of the cabinet* **(Photo 20)**.

Place the 45° end of the moulding to the front edge of the cabinet and then pencil in a straight line on the moulding at the back edge. Make a 90° cut on the miter saw. The trim is glued and nailed to the cabinet, but placement of the glue is important. Do not put glue on the edge of the trim that faces the top. Remember, the top will expand and contract with the seasons. The glue should be placed on the side of the trim that faces the side of the cabinet. The cabinet is made of plywood which is much more stable and the movement will be considerably less **(Photo 21)**. Continue with the stop molding following the same procedure. Make a 45° cut and place it in position on the cabinet. Mark the opposite end and make another cut on the miter saw. Glue and nail the piece into place. Once the stop moulding is done, repeat the procedure for the cove moulding. When nailing, use a nail set to drive the nails in all the way. This will avoid damaging or bruising the moulding.

With the trim all done, turn the cabinet right-side up and mount the doors on the face frame of the cabinet. Use the three-way adjustable screws on the hinges to align the doors and gaps as needed.

The main part of the cabinet is complete; all it needs now are some shelves. The shelves inside the cabinet are 3/4" plywood with a cleat glued and nailed on the front edge. The cleat is a piece of 3/4" x 1". It covers the edges of the plywood and gives it strength to help prevent bowing of the shelf.

With the cabinet sitting on the stand, the last thing to complete the two pieces is the 3/4" quarter-round moulding to go around the bottom. There are two possible options here. You could cut and attached the quarter-rounds to the base of the cabinet. With the cabinet lifted off, you could use the stand as a table by itself if need be. Or, attach the quarter-round to the stand, which will help prevent the cabinet from being bumped or pushed off of the stand. If you decide to attach the quarter-round to the stand, leave a small gap between the cabinet and trim. This will allow the cabinet to be removed easily without any sticking or binding.

Of course the final steps are to sand, stain and apply the finish of your choice to the cabinet and stand. When sanding the solid-wood components, use a series of sandpaper grits beginning with #80 then continue with #100, #150 and #220. However, sanding the plywood sections is different because it has a very thin veneer on the surface. To prevent sanding through the veneer, begin with #150-grit sandpaper then follow up with #220.

Read the directions on the stain and finish to allow proper drying time for each. Apply multiple coats of polyurethane and lightly sand in between each coat with #220-grit sandpaper. The light sanding does two things; one, it removes and minor bumps and raised grain. Two, it roughens the surface up just enough for the next layer of polyurethane to grip and bond to the previous layer.

With it all done, this piece of furniture can find a comfortable place to rest in the home or shop. Inside the house, this project is great for filling it with books, dishes or linens.

And if it's going in the shop, you now have a special goal: Buying some new tools to fill it.

Parts list in inches

QTY.	PART	THICKNESS	WIDTH	LENGTH	NOTES
4	legs	$2\frac{1}{4}$	$2\frac{1}{2}$	28	
2	stand top rails	$\frac{3}{4}$	$5\frac{1}{2}$	25	arched to $3\frac{1}{2}$ at center
2	stand top rails	$\frac{3}{4}$	$5\frac{1}{2}$	$9\frac{3}{4}$	arched to $3\frac{1}{2}$ at center
2	stand bottom rails	$\frac{3}{4}$	$3\frac{1}{2}$	25	
2	stand bottom rails	$\frac{3}{4}$	$3\frac{1}{2}$	$9\frac{3}{4}$	
2	stand & cabinet tops	$\frac{3}{4}$	16	33	
2	cabinet sides	$\frac{3}{4}$	$13\frac{1}{2}$	30	bottom help up $1\frac{1}{2}$
2	cabinet top & bottom	$\frac{3}{4}$	$12\frac{3}{4}$	$28\frac{1}{2}$	
2	cabinet face stiles	$\frac{3}{4}$	$1\frac{1}{2}$	30	
2	cabinet face rails	$\frac{3}{4}$	2	27	
1	cabinet back	$\frac{3}{4}$	$18\frac{1}{2}$	30	
1	shelf(s)	$\frac{3}{4}$	12	$28\frac{1}{2}$	add $\frac{3}{4}$" x 1" strip to front edge
4	door stiles	$\frac{3}{4}$	$2\frac{1}{2}$	27	$\frac{1}{4}$" rabbet for panel
4	door rails	$\frac{3}{4}$	$2\frac{1}{2}$	9	$\frac{1}{4}$" rabbet for panel
2	door panels	$\frac{1}{4}$	$9\frac{1}{2}$	$22\frac{1}{2}$	

approximately 70 lineal inches of each moulding used

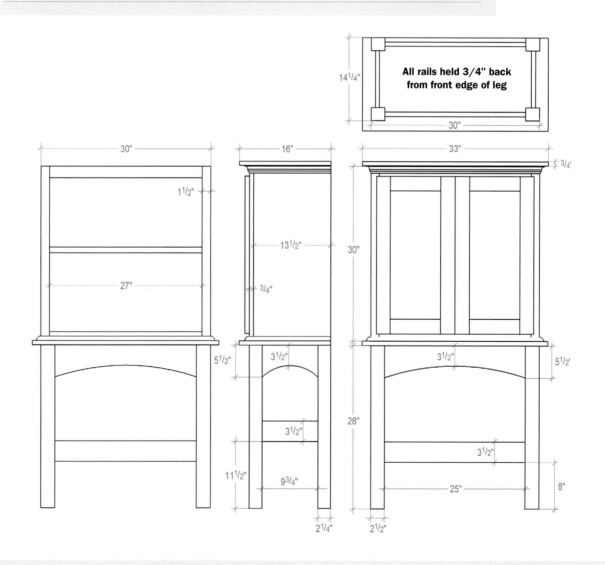

**All rails held 3/4" back
from front edge of leg**

Drop-Front Desk

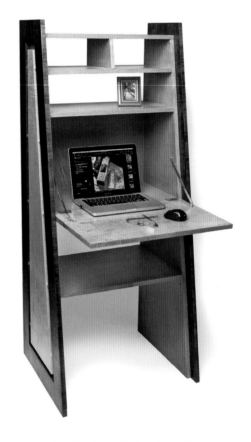

There's something about a drop-front desk I've always liked, but the ones I've always seen remind me of the ones my grandmother used to own. So I designed this one to have a little bit of a modern feel. It is straight at the back, but slopes in the front to give it good, stable visual balance.

The end panels have a two-tone color of natural wood and ebony with aluminum pins connecting them together. For utitility, the desk has a shelf at the top and bottom. And, of course the front drops down to give a nice space for writing, working or, in my case, closes to hide my bills.

The majority of the desk is made from ³/₄" plywood, with hardwood edge banding to hide the cut edges of plywood, plus hardwood trim and accents.

Start by making the desk sides, which are cut on a 10° angle. Refer to the cut list to lay out the cut lines for the sides. Use a circular saw guided with a straightedge or clamp-on fence to cut the side pieces **(Photo 1)**.

With accurate measurements and a straightedge it's still a good idea to make sure both side pieces are exactly the same. Even with a slight difference between the two pieces,

the shelves won't be flush and the drop-front won't close properly. Clamp the sides together and use a handplane to trim the edges even to each other **(Photo 2)**.

To make the shelves all the same length, a miter saw and a stop block would be perfect. However, the shelves are too wide for miter saws to handle. The next best thing is the circular saw crosscutting jig with a straightedge guide that can be clamped across wide boards. Use a clamp and scrap wood for a stop block when setting up the jig, that way all the shelves will come out the same length **(Photo 3)**.

With the shelves cut to length, now cut a 10° bevel on the front edges to match the slanted desk sides.

You could make this with a bevel and handplane, but it's a lot faster and more accurate to use a router in a router table. First mount a flush-cutting bit in the router so that the bearing on the bit is flush with the fence. If the bearing sticks out a tad beyond the fence it will take a more aggressive cut, but it should not stick out too much.

Using a protractor, set a bevel gauge at 10°, then place the stock of the bevel against the router table fence. Use a

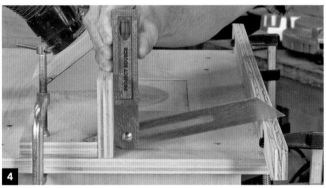

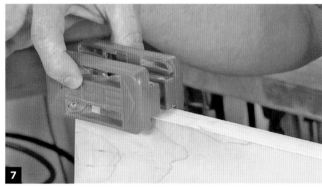

long scrap of wood and move the wood until it just makes contact with the bevel. Then clamp the wood to the router table **(Photo 4)**.

Position the board so it rides on top of the scrap wood and is tight up against the fence and push the board through. This won't remove all the material in one pass, so multiple passes are needed **(Photo 5)**.

With the shelves all beveled, cover the exposed edges with edge banding to hide the layers of plywood and give it the appearance of a solid board. Edge banding is thin hardwood veneer with glue on one face. When heated, the glue melts and bonds the edge banding to the other surface.

To attach the edge banding, begin by cutting a piece slightly longer than the surface to be covered and tape it in place along the plywood edge. The tape prevents the edge banding from curling up as you work. Also, when the glue melts the banding has the tendency to slide around, so the tape helps keep it centered on the wood's edge.

A hot iron does a good job of melting the glue without actually burning the wood or tape. The edge banding packaging will tell you what temperature to set the iron **(Photo 6)**.

Once the banding is on and cooled, remove the tape and trim off the excess banding. The ends can easily be cut off with a razor blade scoring across it. However, the banding is actually wider than the 3/4" wood so it also has to be trimmed to width. Edge-band trimmers have blades with a pair of blades, one on each side. The tool fits over the plywood edge. Squeeze the trimmer and push it along the plywood to trim the banding flush with the edges **(Photo 7)**.

These trimmers do a good job, but it's still a good idea to rub some sandpaper over it to get any sharp, rough edges left behind.

When the banding is complete, begin a partial assembly. Begin with the second shelf and attach the divider. Find the middle of the shelf and drill a couple of pilot holes from the bottom and use screws to secure it in place.

Drill pocket holes through the underside of each of the shelf's ends, then use pocket screws to attach it to the sides. Keep the front of the shelf flush with the front edge of the desk sides. If the shelf is a little too wide, let it stick out at the back and clean it up later with a handplane. Repeat the process to mount the remaining shelves to the side piece **(Photo 8)**.

When attaching the other side piece to the shelves, I found it's a good idea to use pipe or bar clamps to hold the assembly together. Pocket holes are drilled on a slight angle, so when the screws go in they have a tendency to shift the shelf out-of-square. The clamps help prevent this.

Holding a square firmly against the side and shelf, drive the screws into place to secure the shelf **(Photo 9)**.

With the shelves and sides attached, check the assembly for squareness and adjust as needed.

Attaching the desk back will complete this part of the assembly. The back is also held on with pocket screws. It should be precisely cut for a snug fit inside the desk's frame,

then secured with pocket screws from the back side. Once in place, this back adds rigid support to the whole desk unit and helps keep the desk square **(Photo 10)**.

Attach the top with glue and clamps, and then nail it into place.

The front lid, after being cut to size and trimmed with edge banding, is ready to attach. Holding the lid in place while trying to align and screw the hinges on seems as if it requires a third arm, but there is an easier way. On the inner surface of the desk sides, and flush to the desk shelf, clamp two long pieces of scrap wood. This gives support where the lid can rest so the hinges can easily be fastened **(Photo 11)**.

Check to make sure the hinges are operating smoothly and the lid is closing properly. The hinges have small screws in them and cannot fully support the weight of the desk's drop-front lid. For reinforced strength, attach some lid support brackets and check once again that they operate smoothly **(Photos 12)**.

At this point, the main portion of the actual desk is done.

But it's the end panels that give it a modern, contemporary feel, so let's do those next.

The end panels have a center portion of natural maple suspended by aluminum dowel rods inside a trapezoidal frame stained dark. The outer frame, as well as the center portion have a 10° angle at the front. When assembled, the ebony stain on the frame really shows the grain of the center maple wood portion **(Photo 13)**.

We'll construct of the frame, which consists of a rails at the top and bottom and stiles at the front and back, first. Although the measurements are provided on the cut list, instead of cutting them all ahead of time and then assembling them, sometimes it's better to cut each piece as you go to ensure everything fits just right. This way, you can make slight adjustments if you need to.

Cut the rear stile per the cut list. This workpiece is simply cut to length, and is square all the way around.

Use a miter saw to cut the front end of the top rail to 10° on one end, but don't cut it to length yet. Instead, pencil a

light mark on this workpiece where the length should be per the cut list.

Place the top rail on your workbench and lay the rear stile over the top rail at the pencil mark. Use a square to make sure it's at 90° and hold it in place with a clamp **(Photo 14)**.

Repeat the same process for the bottom rail – cut at 10° on front and a pencil mark at the back where it would be cut to join the back stile. Check for square and clamp it securely.

With both the top and bottom rails clamped to the rear stile and both at a true 90°, place the long, uncut front stile in position against the angled ends of the rails. If the stiles meet the rails with no gaps, you're golden **(Photo 16)**.

However, even with careful measuring you may get a slight gap where the stile touches at the rails. In this case it's making contact at the upper edge of the rail, but not at the bottom **(Photo 17)**.

Reasons for this can vary: a bad measurement, your miter saw could be slightly out of calibration, you may have accidentally cut on the wrong side of the pencil line or the wood may be slightly bowed. No matter what happened, if the gap is small there's an easy fix.

Clamp the upper rail end (the one cut at 10°) flush to the front stile. The rear stile on top of the upper rail is already clamped in place, but use a square to make confirm the rear stile is at 90° to the upper rail **(Photo 17)**.

Move to the bottom and clamp the lower rail's 10° end to the front stile. Again, have the rear stile resting on top of the lower rail and make sure that too is at 90° to the rail **(Photo 18)**. Then make a mark with a pencil. You can see that the small pencil line made earlier from the cut list measurements is slightly behind the mark you just made **(Photo 19)**. This will be your new cut line for the lower rail.

With adjustments made, cut the rails and stiles to their final length and you're ready to begin assembling the end pieces.

We'll join the rails and stiles with some 3/8" dowel pins. To make sure that everything lines up, temporarily clamp the assemblies together and make pencil lines crossing over from the stiles to the rails **(Photo 20)**. Also use a number or letter to give that joint a reference so the pieces don't get confused or messed up later.

A doweling jig and a 3/8" drill bit lined up with the pencil marks allows you to drill perfectly perpendicular holes into the workpieces. A stop collar on the drill bit sets the hole at the correct depth. Repeat the same drilling process for all four corners.

The front joints of rails and stiles are angled at 10°, but as long as you align the dowel jig where the line crosses the edges the dowel pins will line up and go together just fine **(Photo 21)**.

There's a lot to go together here – all those dowel pins, aluminum pins, floating center panel – so it's best to approach the glue-up in stages.

We'll start by gluing just the rails to the front stiles. The back rail can be placed in position to add in the clamping process, but don't apply glue to the back stile to the rails yet – remember, we still need to put that floating panel in the middle. *TIP – A scrap piece of wood cut at 10° can be placed on the front of the stile to give a good flat surface for the clamps to squeeze down on. A cutoff from when you cut those rail angles would work perfectly.*

If you haven't already done so, cut the center panel to with

a matching 10° angle on the front. To assist in measuring and marking, set the panel in place with some spacers to keep it centered with equal spacing all around it.

Using the locations on the plans as a guide, draw pencil lines on the back stile where the aluminum pins will go. Use a square to transfer the pencil lines on the rear stile across the center panel and and onto the front stile. Do this for each place the pins will be **(Photo 22)**.

With all the lines made on both stiles and panel, remove the panel from the frame. Use the doweling jig on the back edge of the panel and the front edge of the rear stile to drill 1/2" holes at 1/2" deep. No fancy angle here, so the doweling jig mounts directly on the edge of the wood.

That's not the case for the front edge of the panel, which is angled at 10°. If you place the jig flush on the panel edge the holes will also be on an angle instead of horizontal. The solution is to cut a scrap piece of wood at 10° on the miter saw and place it between the jig and the panel to compensate for the angle. Now you can drill a horizontal hole **(Photo 23)**.

Cut the aluminum pins to size per the cut list, and do a full dry-fit of the end pieces to make sure that everything lines up and fits properly **(Photo 24)**. If all is well, apply glue to the doweled corner joints of the stiles and rails and clamp the assembly up to dry. Do not put any glue on the aluminum pins **(Photo 25)**.

Once both side panels are dry and out of the clamps, give everything a thorough sanding in prepearation for the stain. It's a good idea to do the staining and finishing to the end panels and desk unit while they are separated.

I wanted a dark ebony stain for this project and many

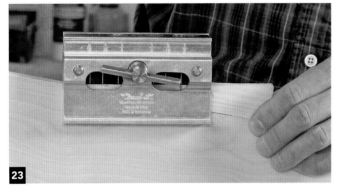

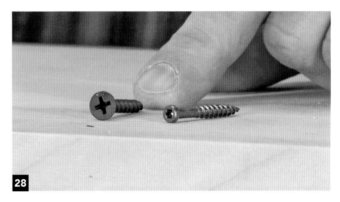

times the color on the can won't match when the stain is applied to the wood **(Photo 26)**. This can be a result of the type of wood the stain is going on or simply the photo on the can is different from the actual stain in the can. So I came up with my own recipe for a dark ebony stain.

The ebony stain on the left is the store brand, and the stain on the right is my homemade formula. To make this rich dark stain I used a can of Minwax ebony stain, mixed in a bottle of calligraphy India ink, and added ¹/₃ of a bottle of violet dye **(Photo 27)**.

After the stain has dried you can apply a clear top coat. Because of the smaller shelves on the desk, it can make it a challenge to get a brush in there. So a wipe-on polyurethane applied with a rag does a nice job of getting into the tight spots. Apply three coats for an even sheen and good protection to the wood.

Once everything is dry, attach the side panels. This is most easily done by simply standing the two side panels up against the sides of the main desk unit. With the bottoms even, center the side panels on the main unit and temporarily clamp them in place.

Drive screws from the inside of the main desk unit to and into the side panels. Even though the screws are on the inside of the desk they can still be noticeable. So instead of regular wood or drywall screws I used some trim screws that have a smaller head to make them less conspicuous **(Photo 28)**.

Parts list in inches

QTY.	PART	THICKNESS	WIDTH	LENGTH
2	sides (ply)	$3/4$	$19^7/8$	$57^1/4$
1	top (ply)	$3/4$	$9^3/4$	24
1	shelf (ply)	$3/4$	$10^3/4$	$22^1/2$
1	shelf (ply)	$3/4$	$11^7/8$	$22^1/2$
1	shelf (ply)	$3/4$	$14^5/8$	$22^1/2$
1	shelf (ply)	$3/4$	$16^7/8$	$22^1/2$
1	divider (ply)	$3/4$	$4^3/4$	$10^3/4$*
1	door (ply)	$3/4$	$16^1/2$*	$23^3/4$
2	frame stiles (solid)	$3/4$	$3^1/2$	60
2	frame stiles (solid)	$3/4$	$3^1/2$	62*
2	frame rails (solid)	$3/4$	$3^1/2$	$14^{13}/16$
2	frame rails (solid)	$3/4$	$3^1/2$	$4^{13}/16$*
20	pegs	$1/2$	$1/2$	2

*cut to fit

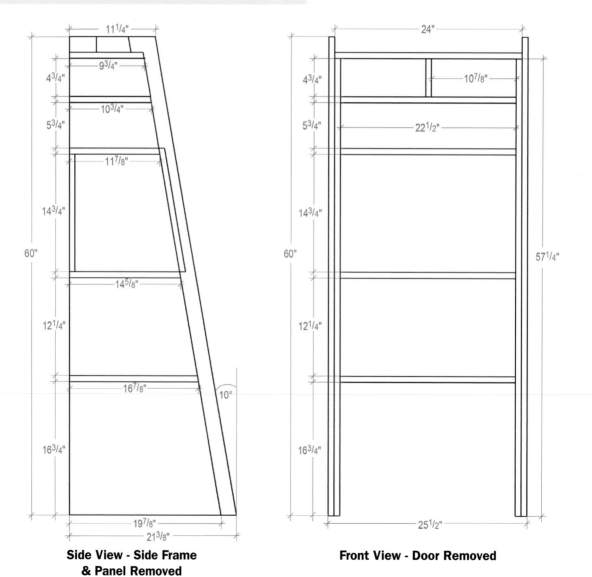

**Side View - Side Frame
& Panel Removed**

Front View - Door Removed

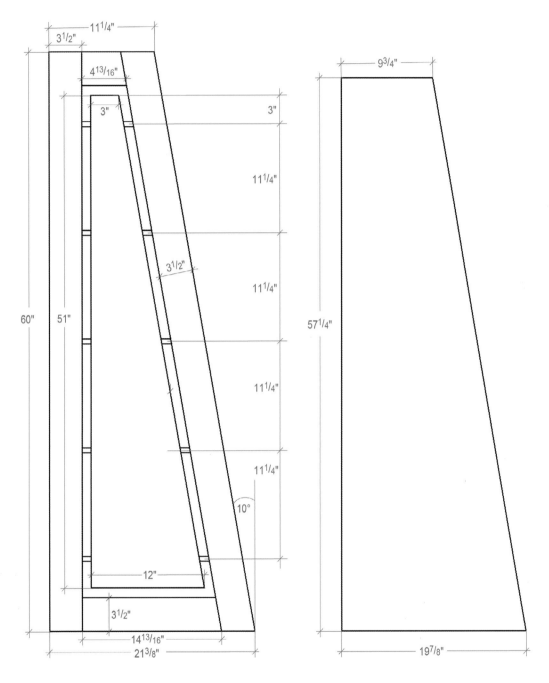

Side Frame

Side Panel

Stackable Storage

Part of my job as a woodworker is keeping myself educated on everything from the ancient traditional methods to current present woodworking techniques. One way I do this is by reading a lot of books. Over the years I've collected a vast number of books, but storage for them has become an issue in my office. So to help me hold my ever-growing collection, I came up with a versatile modular storage unit.

It's a stackable design that allows me to make as many individual boxes as I wish, and they interlock onto each other. The individual modules have simple handles to move them easily from one place to another. You can customize the modules by adding drawers or doors if desired. The stacked unit is finished off with a top cap and bottom base giving it the appearance of a nice-looking bookcase. Best of all, it can be constructed fast and easy.

The top, bottom and two sides of each module are constructed from 1x12 stock and measure 16" in length. Cutting these pieces to exact length is critical for the storage unit to be square and true. If your miter saw is capable of crosscutting boards of this width, use a stop block to make sure each piece comes out the exact same length. If your miter saw can't handle boards this wide, you can make a simple and accurate crosscutting jig for your circular saw **(Photo 1)**.

Once the sides and top are cut, set them aside. However, the bottom piece gets some special attention.

A front 1x2 cleat – which is ³/4" thick – is attached to the leading edge of the board, followed by ¹/4" plywood added to the back edge. Adding these extra pieces means the bottom is about 1" bigger than the sides and top, so you'll have to subtract this measurement from the bottom board to make it even with the sides and top. *NOTE – Not all ¹/4" plywood is a true ¹/4" make sure you measure the thickness of the plywood. Measure and mark the bottom piece by the amount to be cut off.*

Use a jigsaw to rip the bottom board to its new width. Saw on the waste side of your cut line, and use a block plane to shave down to the line. Take your time planing and double-check with a square to make sure the board edge remains square and flat.

The front cleat is the same length as the bottom piece. Cut the 1x2 to length with the miter saw, and then glue and nail the cleat to the edge **(Photo 2)**.

The bottom edges of the sides have notches cut out

for your fingers so you're able to pick up and carry the module. Begin by measuring from the plans and drilling two ³/4" holes at the bottom. *NOTE – Have a sacrificial board underneath the workpiece to prevent drilling into the benchtop.* Then use the jigsaw to cut across the workpiece connecting one hole to the other **(Photo 3)**. Finish by using a file and sandpaper to smooth the underside of any rough edges.

We can begin part of the assembly at this time, fastening the top, bottom and sides with pocket screws. To keep them hidden after the unit is completed, drill the pocket holes on the underside of the top and bottom pieces **(Photo 4)**.

Use some glue and screws and attach one side to the top. It might seem easier to attach the bottom next before the other side, but there is a step that must be done before the bottom goes on. However, temporarily position the bottom in place to help support the other side while you're attaching it.

With the sides and top assembled, let's add a ¹/4" rabbet to the back edge, which will allow the back piece to sit flush

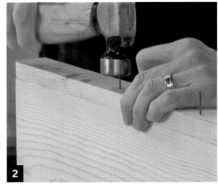
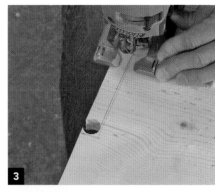

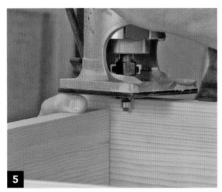

with the sides and top. Make the rabbet with a router and a ¼" rabbeting bit **(Photo 5)**. The reason we haven't yet attached the bottom is because the bearing on the router bit could hit the bottom piece, preventing it from making a full rabbet cut.

Balancing the router on the edge of the workpiece can be tricky, so the workpiece should be securely held in place to prevent it from moving around when routing. Use a couple of wooden screw clamps to hold the unit in place. Rout clockwise around the inside edges of the three pieces.

A router can't make square corners, so once the rabbet cut is done you're still going to have round corners. It's a simple task, though, to square them up with a chisel **(Photo 6)**.

Now, glue and screw the bottom piece in place, creating an open box. To aid in stacking the modules, a bit later we'll add some cleats to the top of each of them so the module above can "lock" into place on the one below for a secure stack. To accommodate these cleats – which are ¾" square stock – inset the bottom by the same amount. Check the unit for squareness. If it's slightly off, the back will help pull the box back into square.

The back is cut from ¼" plywood and nailed in place. Make sure when cutting the plywood that the cuts are straight and square. Use a straightedge when cutting with the circular saw and double-check with a framing square to make sure the corners are a true 90°. A good fit of the back is essential to keep the unit square and true.

That completes one module, but using the same process you can make multiple storage units.

When in their stacked arrangement, the bottom module in the stack rests on a formal base. In fact, it actually fits inside the bottom base, so we'll make the base a little larger than the modules.

Crosscut the front, back and sides of the bottom base to length from 1x4 stock. Although the measurements are given in the plans, it's a good idea to get the size from of the modules you just made to assure a proper fit.

At 3½", the back piece is a too wide, so cut it down to 2" with a the jigsaw, then clean up the cut with the block plane. Pocket-screw the sides to the front and the back to the sides. Drill pocket holes and use glue when attaching with the screws.

With the basic frame of the base formed, attach cleats on the inside to support the bottom module of the stack. The cleats are ¾" stock, glued and screwed ¾" from the top edge of the two sides. This shallow inset allows the storage module to lock into the base and also hide the handle notches.

To dress up the base, wrap some 3¼" baseboard around it. Begin by cutting the ends of the baseboard at 45° with a miter saw. Place the baseboard to the side of the base unit. The heal of the miter cut is placed at the front corner of the base. *TIP – Shade the heel edge of the miter cut with a pencil. This makes it easier to see when lining it up to the corner edge* **(Photo 7)**.

With the miter cut in place at the front corner, mark the back edge on the trim and make the straight cut on the miter saw.

Take the side piece of trim and hold it in place with some spring clamps on the base. Take the remaining baseboard and make the mating miter cut to form the front piece. Check the fit on the two mitered pieces. If it looks good,

mark with the pencil and cut the miter for the second corner **(Photo 8)**.

TIP – instead of trying to cut exactly to the line on the first try, cut the miter a little proud on the waste side and then slowly sneak up on the line to make a good fit.

Place the front trim to the base, hold it with spring clamps and repeat the process to make the final side trim piece **(Photo 9)**. Once the pieces are all cut and looks like a good fit, glue and nail the trim pieces to the base.

Test how the modules fit into the bottom base. Sometimes a little planing or sanding is needed so each storage module easily fits inside the base.

The top cap is made up of a 1x10 and a 1x4 glued together. When clamping the boards for gluing, leave the overall length of the boards a little long. Sometimes the boards can shift during the clamping procedure. With the boards left long you can crosscut to length in the circular saw jig after the panel has dried.

With the top dry and out of the clamps, add some ¾ square stock to the underside that acts as a stop to position it correctly atop the stacked storage unit. The stock is simply glued and nailed in place. However, some ¹¹/₁₆" cove molding will go in front of the stock to help dress up the finished look of the piece. The cove molding is cut at 45° on the miter saw and the same procedure is used for the cove molding as the baseboards.

The top cap is finished, but before you can start stacking everything one more thing is needed. On each of the storage modules, glue and nail some ³/₄" square stock on the top of each unit **(Photo 10)**.

Attached to the sides, these act as cleats that interlock with either the next storage module or the top cap being placed on it. Each of the ³/₄" cleats has the corner ends beveled at 45°. This just aids it in easier alignment when the next module is set on top. When stacking the modules, you can see the need for insetting the bottom earlier by ³/₄" to accommodate these cleats.

For the most part, the stackable storage unit is done. Adding some simple doors or drawers is another way to customize it and can help to hide some unsightly clutter. But neither is necessary. All that is left is some sanding and the finish.

I used a whitewash stain on the finished modules. This stain adds some color, but unlike white paint it still allows the wood grain to show. I used two coats of stain to achieve the depth of color I desired. For the top coat, I used a water-based polyurethane. Unlike an oil-based polyurethane, water-based poly dries fast and is perfectly clear, without the slightly "yellow" hue oil-based poly sometimes has.

I love this stackable storage unit because I continually move it around, and add to it because it's totally customizable. Best of all, it give me another reason to keep buying more books.

Parts list in inches

QTY.	PART	THICKNESS	WIDTH	LENGTH	NOTES
FOR 1 CENTER MODULE					
2	sides	3/4	11 1/4	16	notched for handle
1	bottom	3/4	10 1/4	16	
1	front rail	3/4	1 1/2	16	
1	top	3/4	11 1/4	16	
1	back	1/4	16 1/2	15 1/2	
2	guides	3/4	1	9 3/4	
2	doors	3/4	8	13 3/4	optional, cut to fit
TOP MODULE					
1	top	3/4	12 3/4	20 1/2	
	cove moulding	3/4	3/4	48	base moulding
BASE MODULE					
2	sides	3/4	3 1/2	11 1/4	
2	front	3/4	3 1/2	19	
2	back	3/4	2	17 1/2	
2	cleats	3/4	3/4	11 1/4	
2	cleat	3/4	3/4	16	
	base moulding	1/2	3 1/4	48	

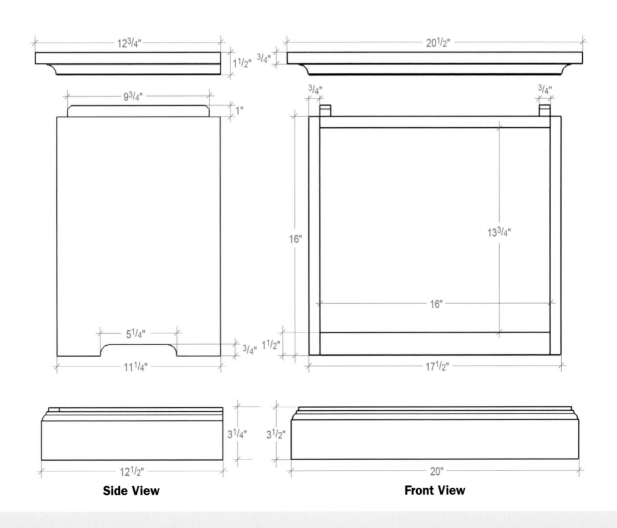

Side View   **Front View**

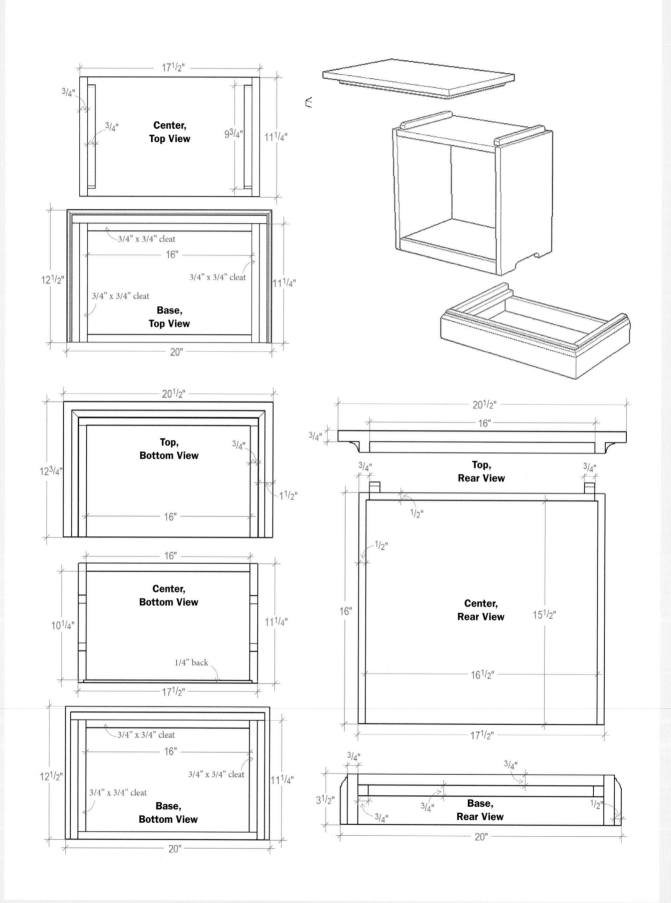

Center,
Top View

17½"

3/4"

3/4"

9¾"

11¼"

Base,
Top View

3/4" x 3/4" cleat

16"

3/4" x 3/4" cleat

3/4" x 3/4" cleat

12½"

11¼"

20"

Top,
Bottom View

20½"

12¾"

3/4"

16"

1½"

Center,
Bottom View

16"

10¼"

11¼"

1/4" back

17½"

Base,
Bottom View

3/4" x 3/4" cleat

16"

3/4" x 3/4" cleat

3/4" x 3/4" cleat

12½"

11¼"

20"

Top,
Rear View

20½"

16"

3/4"

Center,
Rear View

3/4"

3/4"

1/2"

1/2"

16"

15½"

16½"

17½"

Base,
Rear View

3/4"

3/4"

3½"

3/4"

3/4"

1/2"

20"

Fireplace Bookcase

Being a professional furniture maker, I get a lot of requests for fireplace mantels. However, depending on where you live the codes and requirements can vary, making it difficult to design a fireplace mantel that universally meets safety codes. On top of that, some folks may not even have a fireplace. So I came up with the fireplace bookcase.

This project looks like a fireplace mantel. It has the base, columns and a top. But in the middle are shelves making it perfect for books or any other knickknacks you might have.

The bookcase is made from dimensional lumber with very little need to cut down any boards except to length, and the majority of the lumber is crosscut and pocket screwed together. To help dress it up some I added baseboards at the bottom and crown moulding up top.

Begin by making the base. The top of the base is a 4' length of standard 1x12 that requires no cutting at all. Make sure that the piece is nice and flat, and not bowed, warped or twisted in any way.

The front and sides of the base are made from standard 1x6 boards cut to length from the dimensions on the cut list. Pocket screw the sides to the front and also pocket screw it to the base top **(Photo 1)**.

After attaching the fronts and sides to the top, turn the base right-side up and get ready to add some baseboards around it. A 6' piece of baseboard from the big box store cut into sections will easily go around the base.

Begin with the baseboard that will go on the front. At the miter saw, cut a 45° bevel at one end. Place the baseboard on the front with the back side of the bevel cut coming to the edge of the front corner.

Then at the opposite end, mark a pencil line on the back side of the baseboard where it comes into contact with the corner **(Photo 2)**.

Set your miter saw at 45° in the opposite direction of the first cut. The pencil line is on the back side of the baseboard,

which may make it hard to see. *TIP – Cut the board a little long and then slowly sneak up on the line.*

Glue and nail the front baseboard to the base. Then bevel one end of a side baseboard at 45° and place it tightly against the mitered corner of the front baseboard **(Photo 3)**. With a pencil, mark on the baseboard where it comes to the back of the base, then make a straight cut with the miter saw on your line to cut the side pieces to length. Glue and nail them on.

The base is completed and can be set aside.

The fireplace column frames are cut to length from standard 1x2, 1x4 and 1x6 stock.

The 1x4 and 1x6 will be the rails on these columns and are cut to a length of 4" **(Photo 4)**. It is important that they are cut the same so the column, when glued up, is square.

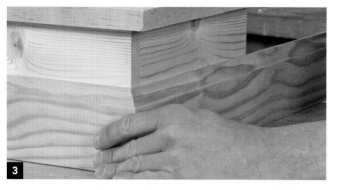

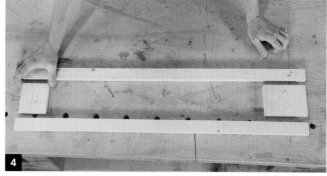

To assure each piece is cut to the same length, use a stop block on the miter saw. Use the same procedure to cut the 1x2 stiles to the exact same length.

The 1x4 and 1x6 workpieces receive some pocket holes and screws to attach the 1x2 stiles **(Photo 5)**.

After the column frames are glued and screwed together, cut the center panels to size per the cut list from 1/4" plywood. Make sure the panels overlap the frame openings by at least 3/4". Then attach the panel to the back of the column frames with some glue and brads **(Photo 6)**.

Cut the sides for the columns to length from standard 1x10, and pocket-screw them to the back edges of the column frames **(Photo 7)**.

To enclose the column, cut a top and bottom from 1x10, sized to fit inside the column. Slide these pieces into place and secure them with glue and nails **(Photo 8)**. Repeat the process for the second column.

The mantel top that rests on the columns is larger than a dimensional piece of lumber you'll find at the store, and is glued up from a 1x12 and 1x4, then rip cut to 13 1/4" wide.

Rip cut the board with the jigsaw and clean up the edge with a block plane.

Cut the front and sides for the mantel top to size per the cut list, and attach them to the underside of the top in the same manner as the base. Essentially, the top is an upside-down version of the base at this point, just a little wider **(Photo 9)**.

Unlike the 6' baseboard you used for the fireplace base, you'll need to buy a little more than 6' of crown moulding. The reason for this is that for on the baseboard, the wood sits flat against the base and the miter cuts are small **(Photo 10)**.

However, the crown moulding is cut at a compound angle, making the miter cut – and the material needed – a bit longer **(Photo 11)**.

A compound miter saw is typically the tool of choice for cutting crown moulding, as the tool pivots at the front and also tilts at the back. However, you can cut this basic crown moulding with a regular miter saw. First, turn the miter saw to 45°. Then, instead of placing the moulding flat against the saw fence or table, angle it against both in the same orientation it'll be in when mounted, with the two narrow edges resting evenly

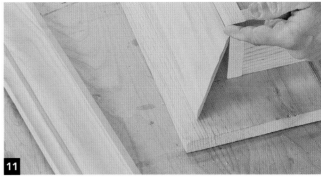

on the back fence and the table **(Photo 12)**.

Hold the crown moulding tightly against the fence. Then, making sure your hand is out of the way of the blade, make the cut.

The cutting produced is just like that of the baseboards – formed on one end only, and not yet cut to length. Cut the front piece and hold it in place at one the corner. At the other corner mark the back of the crown moulding. Change the angle on the miter saw to the opposite 45° direction. Slowly make a series of cuts sneaking up on the pencil line.

Before cutting the sides, nail the front crown moulding into place. This can be tricky, however, because there's very little contacting surface to be nailed through. You can make nailing easier by filling in the void behind the crown moulding. Hold a piece of scrap crown moulding against the mantel top. Now, chamfer one corner of a length of 1x2 just enough so it fits behind the crown moulding **(Photo 13)**.

Glue and nail the 1x2 across the front and sides of the mantel top, and use it as a backing on which you can more easily nail the crown moulding.

For the side mouldings, cut the 45° miter on a long piece of crown moulding just as you did for the front. Hold the side crown in position and mark with a pencil where it hits the back of the mantel top. Then cut it to length with a straight cut on the miter saw **(Photo 14)**.

The top is almost done, but it still needs a bottom to attach the side columns to. Cut the bottom to size to fit neatly inside the mantel top **(Photo 15)**, and support it with a couple of spacer blocks while you drive pocket screws into place at the ends and front.

The two bookcase shelves are standard 1x10s cut to length, with pocket holes drilled on the underside at both ends. The front of each shelf receives a piece of 1x2 trim that is glued and nailed into place **(Photo 16)**.

Now cut the decorative arch for the top of the fireplace opening from a piece of 1x4 the same length as the shelves. From the plans, make a template and trace it onto the 1x4, then cut it out with a jigsaw and smooth the edges. Drill a pair of pocket holes at each end of the inner surface of the arch **(Photo 17)**.

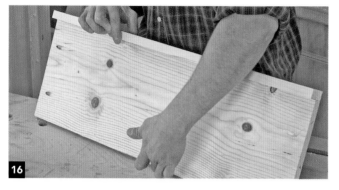

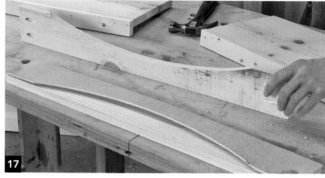

Before beginning assembly, cut some scrap plywood so the piece length equals the distance between the shelves. Set the columns upright on your workbench and, starting from the bottom, clamp the plywood to the inside bottoms of the columns. Now you can rest the shelf firmly on the scrap plywood supports as you pocket-screw the shelf into place from underneath **(Photo 18)**.

Repeat the process for the next shelf. Note that I wanted the spacing of the second shelf to be different from the first, so I used a different-sized scrap of plywood as a spacer between the two shelves. You can vary the spacing of the shelves any way you like by simply cutting the plywood spacers accordingly.

With the shelves attached, lay the whole unit face down on your worksurface to install the top arch. The arch piece doesn't sit flush with the front of the columns. It sits back 3/4" forming a reveal. Place scraps of 3/4" wood down on the worksurface and then place the arch atop that, then pocket-screw the arch to the columns **(Photo 19)**.

Complete the main assembly by attaching the mantel top. Turn the whole mantel upside down and place it on the inverted top section. From the backside, drill a couple

of clearance holes through the top of the column and then screw it to the top. Do this on each column **(Photo 20)**.

Now flip the whole mantel right-side up, and set it on the base. The base is attached in the same manner as the top – a couple of clearance holes in the bottom of the columns and then screwed solidly to the base.

Finally, cut some 1/4" plywood and then simply screw it to the back opening of the mantel assembly **(Photo 21)**.

The construction is all done and the decision to paint or stain it comes into mind. Since I made this project out of number two grade pine, I chose to paint it to cover up the knots and imperfections in the wood. However, because I'm using a semi-gloss paint, the higher glossy sheen will highlight any missed sanding marks left behind. So extra attention to detail is needed when sanding.

If you make your fireplace bookcase out of an attractive hardwood, such as oak or cherry, a clear polyurethane would be your best finish choice.

Once the fireplace bookcase is completed it will make any room look more sophisticated and charming.

Parts list in inches

QTY.	PART	THICKNESS	WIDTH	LENGTH
1	top	$3/4$	$13^{1}/4$	51
2	mantel sides	$3/4$	$3^{1}/2$	$9^{1}/4$
1	mantel bottom	$3/4$	$9^{1}/4$	$43^{1}/2$
1	mantel front	$3/4$	$3^{1}/2$	45
1	facia board	$3/4$	$3^{1}/2$	$29^{1}/2$*
1	base top	$3/4$	$11^{1}/4$	48
2	base sides	$3/4$	$5^{1}/2$	$9^{1}/4$
1	base front	$3/4$	$5^{1}/2$	46
4	post sides	$3/4$	$9^{1}/4$	$37^{1}/2$
4	post vertical trim	$3/4$	$1^{1}/2$	$37^{1}/4$
2	post top trim	$3/4$	$3^{1}/2$	4
2	post bottom trim	$3/4$	$5^{1}/2$	4
2	post trim backs	$1/4$	$5^{1}/2$	36
4	post tops & bottoms	$3/4$	$5^{1}/2$	$9^{1}/4$
2	shelves	$3/4$	$9^{1}/4$	$29^{1}/2$
2	shelf front edges	$3/4$	$1^{1}/2$	$29^{1}/2$
1	back	$1/4$	31	39
1	crown molding	$1/2$	$3^{1}/4$	96**
1	crown blocking	$3/4$	$1^{1}/2$	96**
1	base molding	$1/2$	$3^{1}/4$	96**

*shape to fit

**cut to length to fit

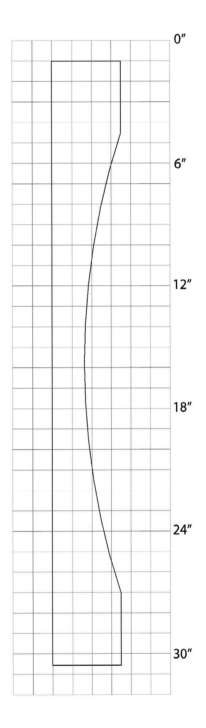

Facia Pattern
1 square = 1"

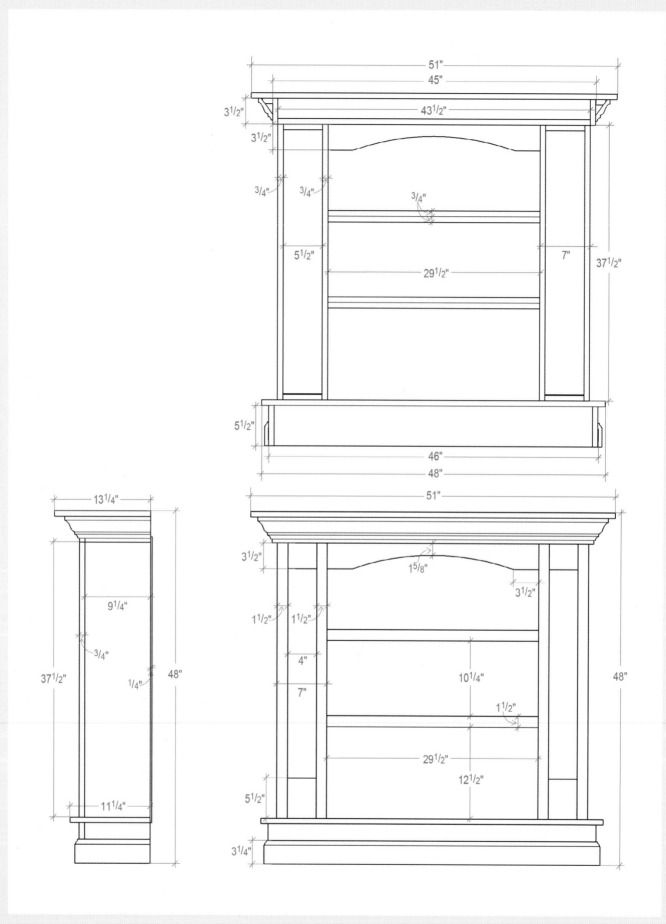

Shaker Wall Box

The Shakers were a religious group founded in the 18th century that reached its peak in the mid-1800s. One of the things they were known for was their high-quality furniture. Everything had a purpose and a specific place. One such piece was the wall box. This could hang on a wall as the name implies, rested on a fireplace mantel or carried anywhere it was needed. With a small drawer and a lid made with cotter-pin hinges, it held small items such as matches, spices or anything else they wanted to place out of sight. This design is still useful today and is perfect on the desk to hold pens, tape and other small miscellaneous items.

To make a wall box begin with the back, which we'll cut out of a 1x12 pine board. Use a compass to create the scalloped shape, or another pattern that suits your fancy. With the shape drawn on the board, cut it out with a jigsaw **(Photo 1)**.

The jigsaw leaves some pretty rough edges left behind on the wood, so a rasp and sandpaper will clean it up nicely.

The box front and sides, as well as the drawer front, are all 1x4 pine cut to length from the plans. Temporarily clamp the drawer front and sides to the back. Then place the front in position. I used some laminate samples I had lying around – these are free at any big box store – and placed them in between the box front and drawer front giving it a little space. Lacking these, you can use anything that's about 1/16" thick to set this gap.

There is an angle at the top of the two side pieces that pitches down in the front. With a ruler, draw a line going from the corner edge of the side down to the corner edge of the front piece **(Photo 2)**.

Remove the clamp and the side pieces and cut the angle on a miter saw. To find the angle, use a bevel gauge and set it to the pencil line drawn on the workpieces.

Place the bevel stock against the miter saw fence and turn the saw's blade to match the angle set on the bevel.

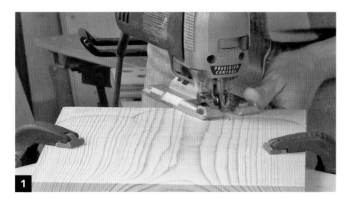

1

2

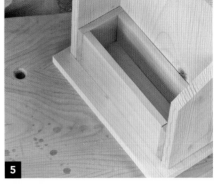

Lock the blade in place and make the cut. *TIP – Cut both side pieces at the same time to assure they're equal in length.*

For the box front, transfer lines from the edge along the face and then to the opposite side of the workpiece **(Photo 3)**. Then place the workpiece in a vise and use a block plane and shave down to the line.

Some assembly is next. Drill pilot holes in the back with a 1/16" drill bit, then glue and nail the sides on **(Photo 4)**. TIP – Balancing the sides to drive a nail in can be awkward. So use the vise or clamp on one of the side pieces to give it a wider base.

Now, drill, glue and nail the bottom on.

The basic structure of the wall box is done and the drawer is next. The drawer is made up of 1/2" x 3 1/2" poplar. Most big box stores carry hardwood in craft sizes, so you should be able to find the poplar in this thickness easily. Place one squared-off length of poplar inside the box and mark the depth from the side of the box itself.

Cut the two sides for the drawer on the miter saw. Place

them back into position inside the wall box and then take the measurement between them for both the front and back pieces, and cut them to length on the miter saw **(Photo 5)**.

The drawer bottom is also made from 1/2" poplar, and is the same length as the front and back, but because it fits inside the sides, it must be ripped to size. Again use the drawer itself to determine the proper width and use a jigsaw and block plane to make it the correct width.

The drawer construction at this point is fairly straightforward. Drill pilot holes for nails in the sides, and use glue before nailing it all together.

With the drawer assembled, test the fit in the box. Then attach the drawer front to the drawer by applying glue to the back of the drawer front and hold it to the drawer with spring clamps. *NOTE – Make sure the drawer front edges are flush with the sides of the wall box* **(Photo 6)**.

Then remove the drawer unit and nail the drawer front in place **(Photo 7)**.

Once the drawer front is attached, set the drawer back into the wall box as a guide for installing a divider between the two sections. To help prevent the drawer from sticking on the divider, use the spacers again to set the divider height, and then nail the divider in place through the sides **(Photo 8)**. Then, with the spacers still in place, glue and nail the front on **(Photo 9)**.

Next is the lid. As mentioned in the beginning, the hinge for the lid is a couple of cotter pins. One pair of pins will go straight into the lid while another pair of pins goes through the back and then the legs are bent over to lock them in place **(Photo 10)**.

Before installing the cotter pin hinges, chamfer the rear edge of the lid. This chamfer allows the lid to open wider

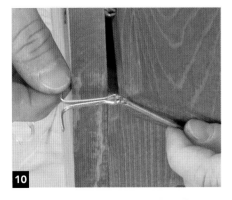

for easy access inside the wall box storage area. With a block plane, shave the corners off the edge of the board creating the chamfer **(Photo 11)**.

Set the cotter pins into the lid first. The cotter pin here is 1/8" in size, so the pilot hole **(Photo 12)** drilled is one size down (7/64") to allow the wood to compress a little as the pin goes in and holds it snuggly in place so as to not fall out.

Place the lid in position on the wall box. Sight down from the top and mark on the back of the wall box where the cotter pin holes will go **(Photo 13)**.

Change drill bits to an 1/8" and then drill through the back of the wall box.

With a hammer, tap the cotter pins into the rear edge of the lid piece **(Photo 14)**.

Once both cotter pins are into the lid, slip the second set of pins through the loop on the first set **(Photo 15)**.

Put the lid back into position on the wall box and slide the cotter pins through the holes on the back. Then spread the cotter pins out by bending over the exposed tips of the pins to lock them in place. **(Photo 16)**.

Final touches for the wall box is drilling a hole at the top to hang it on the wall, and adding a knob on the front for the drawer.

Be sure to sand the project, then stain and finish it to any color desired.

This is a fun project and the shapes and designs for it are almost endless. The Shakers may no longer be around today, but the types of furniture they made can still live on and have a purpose for years to come.

Parts list in inches

QTY.	PART	THICKNESS	WIDTH	LENGTH	NOTES
1	back	$3/4$	$11^1/_4$	14	
2	sides	$3/4$	$3^1/_2$	$9^5/_{16}$	32.5° angle top
1	bottom	$3/4$	$5^1/_2$	$12^1/_4$	
1	lid	$3/4$	$5^1/_2$	$12^1/_4$	
1	front	$3/4$	$3^1/_2$	$11^1/_4$	32.5° bevel top
1	drawer front	$3/4$	$3^1/_2$	$11^1/_4$	
2	drawer sides	$3/4$	$3^1/_2$	$3^1/_2$	
2	drawer F & B	$3/4$	$3^1/_2$	$8^3/_4$	
1	drawer bottom	$3/4$	$2^1/_2$	$8^3/_4$	

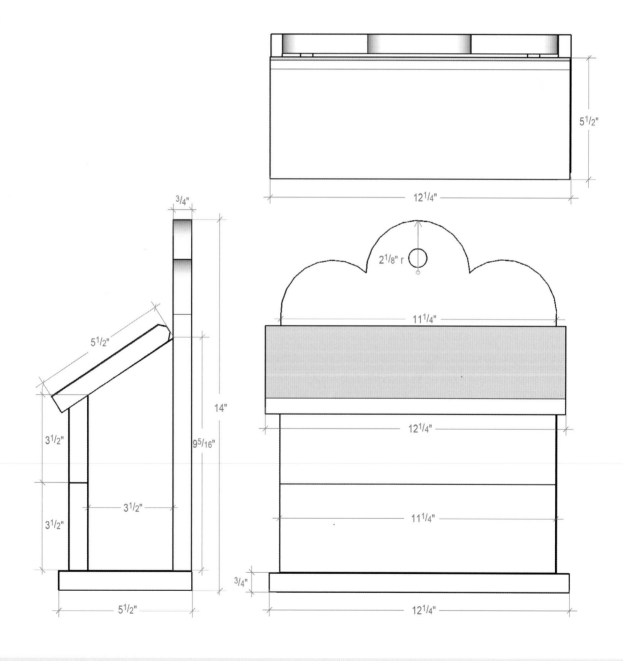

Oak Hall Mirror

Everyone wants to look good. Whether it's getting dressed for the day, or just adjusting your tie before heading out for dinner, we all want to look respectable as we greet the world. This oak hall mirror is a great way to help to do that. It's fashioned in the Arts & Crafts style using a wide top piece supported by decorative brackets. It has trim around the frame of the mirror that helps create shadow lines and give more dimension to the overall look.

It includes two rabbet-constructed drawers to hold small items. Below the drawers are some hooks, ideal for hanging coats, ties or keys. This hall mirror is functional enough for the entryway or the mudroom, but is handsome enough to look at home in the bedroom.

It should be noted that the mirror in this project was custom-sized to fit this frame. If you have a mirror of your own, or purchased one at a store, you may need to alter the frame size of the project, or have the mirror professionally cut.

Also, keep in mind that oak is a very hard wood, so it's important to drill pilot holes for all fasteners, especially nails, to make driving them easier and to prevent splitting.

Begin construction with the upper frame for the mirror. Cut the 1x4 to length from the dimensions in the plans. We'll use pocket screws for the frame joinery, but before drilling, take note where the pocket screws will go. There's a rabbet on the inside edges to allow the mirror to set in. So to be on the safe side, mark the location of the holes so as not to interfere with the rabbet **(Photo 1)**.

Use pocket screws to assemble the frame **(Photo 2)**.

To make the rabbet on the back, use a router with a 3/8" rabbeting bit. The bit has a guide bearing to prevent burn marks left behind on the wood when spinning, and from the side of the bearing to the cutting tip measures 3/8", which creates a rabbet of that width. The depth of the rabbet is determined by setting the bit to 1/4" below the base of the router **(Photo 3)**.

Before using the router, proper direction of the router is necessary for it to perform effectively. A good rule of thumb is; when routing on the inside of a workpiece go clockwise. If I was going to put the rabbet on the outside of the frame I would have gone counterclockwise.

The router does most of the job making the rabbet, however the corners remain round. Use a chisel to square up each corner **(Photo 4)**.

The rabbet is a 1/4" deep but the mirror is only 1/8" thick.

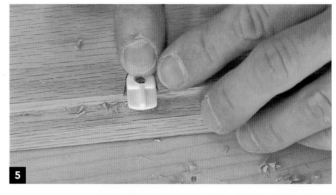

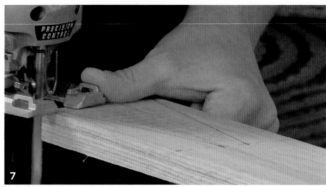

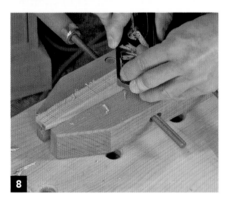

The other ⅛" is going made up by the clips holding the mirror in place. The clips are some screen door hardware. Use a Forstner bit slightly wider than the clips and countersink ⅛" into the frame. Make sure to use several clips all around the frame to adequately hold the mirror in place (Photo 5).

Now, turn the frame over to attach additional trim to the outside edges on the sides and the top. But before adding the trim, sand the frame – it's easier to do now versus after the trim is added. Cut the trim pieces to length for the sides, and glue and nail them on. Place the top piece of trim between the two side pieces and mark the piece to length. *TIP – This is a more accurate and faster way to fit a piece than measuring* (Photo 6).

Then cut the trim to length on the miter saw, and glue and nail it in place.

Next are the little brackets that will hold the top piece. These brackets are long, thin and angled. Cutting small pieces with a power tool can be dangerous. Instead, measure out the pieces on a long board, then clamp it to

your workbench and cut the angles with a jigsaw (Photo 7).

Unclamp the board and crosscut the brackets to length on the miter saw.

Complete the bracket by using a block plane to remove any saw marks left behind from the jigsaw (Photo 8).

To mount the brackets to the frame, trace around them and then drill clearance holes for screws to go through (Photo 9). Pay attention to the placement of the holes and the length of screws used. Remember that the bracket is tapered, so be careful that the screw doesn't come all they way through the front of the bracket.

With both brackets on the frame, glue and nail a piece of ¾" square stock between them for added detail (Photo 10).

The top is a piece of 1x4, cut to length. Place the top in position making sure it's centered with equal distances at both ends. With a pencil, trace around the brackets onto the underside of the top piece, then drill ¹⁄₁₆" pilot holes where the 1¼" nails will go.

It's a good idea to use glue when nailing on the top piece

With the rabbet cut made, rip the sides down to proper width with a jigsaw and then smooth it up with a block plane. From there, cut each individual side to length on the miter saw. Take note of the middle divider dimensions. It is smaller in height and width than the side pieces.

Cut the 1/4" plywood back to size, then drill pilot holes and assemble the sides, middle divider, bottom and back with glue and nails **(Photo 12)**.

It might be tempting to nail the top shelf piece on now, but saving that for later makes it easier to see and fit the drawers. So making the drawers is the next logical step.

These drawers have a 1/2" deep and 3/8" wide rabbet joint on them. The rabbet joint is stronger than a typical butt joint. The rabbet has a shoulder on the one side of the workpiece that helps prevent racking and gives some extra gluing surface **(Photo 13)**.

You could use the router as before, but another method is to cut the rabbets with a pullsaw.

Begin by cutting the face of the drawer to the size of the drawer opening. *NOTE – For a more accurate fit, it's better to work from your actual project size than to cut this dimension from the plans.*

Place the drawer front face down on the workbench. Place the 1/2" poplar drawer side on the drawer front flush to its side. With a sharp pencil, draw a line on the drawer front **(Photo 14)**.

Then place the drawer front in a vise, and set a combination square to 3/8" and draw a line lengthwise on the end grain **(Photo 15)**.

Shade the area to be removed with a pencil so as not to confuse the area to be cut away.

Place the workpiece on the bench and clamp another

to prevent it from coming off if someone was to pick the hall mirror up from the top. When the top is glued and nailed onto the frame, it can be set aside.

Before starting the lower section, take note of the side pieces. The sides should have the edge grain facing forward, not the end grain. If end grain faced out, the stain would absorb more and the look of the project would not be pleasing. The edge grain will give it a better, more uniformed look.

The 1x6 sides also receive a 1/4" deep by 1/4" wide rabbet on the back edge so the back panel sits flush when time to assemble. Cutting a rabbet on the edge of a small piece with a router is difficult because the workpiece isn't wide enough to support the router base when making the cut. But there is a safer way to make this rabbet cut.

Clamp a piece of 2x6 face-to-face with a long 1x6 workpiece for the sides with a wooden handscrew clamp. Then use another clamp to fasten the handscrew to your benchtop. Now the router has a wider base to rest on so you can safely make the cut **(Photo 11)**.

wider board to it. Place the wide board right on the line to be cut. This board will act as a fence for the pullsaw to help keep the saw upright and straight **(Photo 16)**.

Keep the saw flat against the wide board and make the crosscut on the line. Check often to make sure the saw stays on the line and doesn't cut too deep **(Photo 17)**.

With the crosscut done, place the drawer front upright in the vise to cut the other half of the rabbet. Starting the cut is tricky so begin on the corner. Once the cut is started keep an eye on the line of both the end grain and edge grain to make sure the saw is staying on the line. Work the saw down the edge grain first. Then slowly tilt the saw forward and carefully cut the line going along the end grain **(Photo 18)**.

Slowly tilt the saw forward and cut to about the middle on the end grain. Then turn the board around and do the same procedure from the other corner.

Work slowly and carefully to join the two cut lines together.

Once the section is cut out, sight down the rabbet to make sure it's square. It might need a little clean up. If so, use a chisel to remove any high spots or unwanted material. Repeat the process for the matching rabbet at the other end of the drawer front.

Cut the sides, back and bottom to size, then glue and nail them in place **(Photo 19)**. Double-check the size and fit of these pieces to the drawer opening to make sure it's flush and moves easily.

The lower section is two brackets with a piece of 1x4 in between them **(Photo 20)**. These brackets are made the same way as the brackets holding the top. To attach the brackets to the 1x4, make sure to first drill pilot holes, then glue and nail the brackets to the ends of the 1x4.

Center the lower section to the drawer unit and make sure there is equal distance on both sides of the brackets. Trace around the brackets with a pencil on the bottom side

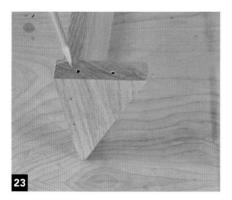

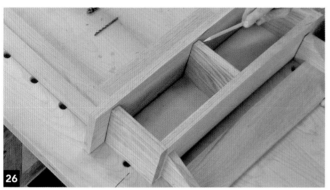

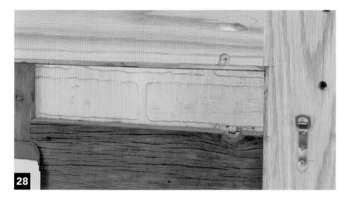

of the drawer unit **(Photo 21)**.

From the bottom, drill a couple of clearance holes through the drawer unit and countersink the holes on the top side so the screws are flush and won't interfere with the drawer when it slides in **(Photo 22)**.

Place the bracket assembly back in place and drill a couple of pilot holes to prevent splitting the brackets **(Photo 23)**. Then screw the brackets on.

Use screws to attach the shelf to the upper frame. Drill clearance holes through the shelf, then drill pilot holes up into the frame. Countersink the holes on the underside of the shelf so the screw heads sit flush and are hidden from view **(Photo 24)**.

Then glue and screw the shelf to the frame **(Photo 25)**.

To attach the lower section, center and position the section to the shelf and trace around the drawer sides and middle divider on the underside of the shelf **(Photo 26)**. Using screws

from the top to attach the lower section would not be very attractive, so a better option is glue and nails.

Drill $1/16$" pilot holes in the penciled area on the underside of the shelf.

Then clamp the upper unit and lower section together, and use glue and $11/2$" 4d nails to fasten them together. The nails heads are small and barely noticeable from the top **(Photo 27)**.

The bulk of the work is done. Sand, stain and finish your mirror and then add the hooks and the knobs for the drawers. Attaching them is straightforward, but once again it's a good idea to drill pilot holes for the hardware. Finally, add some some strap hangers on the back to mount the mirror on the wall **(Photo 28)**.

Hanging this mirror, or any picture, with two individual nails is tricky, so here is a tip.

Measure the distance between the two strap hooks on the back side of the mirror, and mark that distance on a straight scrap piece of wood. Place two screws through the scrap wood so they just barely poke out the other side of the board. Place the scrap board on the wall at the desired location to be hung, using a level to make sure it's not tilted. Then press firmly against the board. It will leave two small dimples in the wall where the hanging screws go.

NOTE – If the screws do not hit wall studs, make sure to use adequate wall anchors to support the weight of the hall mirror.

Your new mirror will look great anywhere in the house. Best of all, whenever you get dressed up you can look into a mirror that has a lot of style of its own.

Parts list in inches

QTY.	PART	THICKNESS	WIDTH	LENGTH	NOTES
2	frame verticals	$3/4$	$3^1/2$	$32^3/4$	$1/4$ x $1/4$ rabbet
2	frame tops & bottom	$3/4$	$3^1/2$	$15^1/2$	$1/4$ x $1/4$ rabbet
2	vertical trim pieces	$1/4$	$1^1/2$	$32^3/4$	
1	horizontal trim piece	$1/4$	$1^1/2$	$19^1/2$	
1	square trim piece	$3/4$	$3/4$	20	
2	top brackets	$3/4$	$1^1/2$	6	cut to shape
1	top	$3/4$	$3^1/2$	$26^1/2$	
2	drawer box sides	$3/4$	5	$5^1/2$	$1/4$ x $1/4$ rabbet
1	drawer box top	$3/4$	$5^1/2$	$26^1/2$	
1	drawer box bottom	$3/4$	5	21	
1	drawer box back	$1/4$	$4^3/4$	$21^1/2$	
4	drawer sides	$1/2$	$4^1/2$	$4^5/8$	
2	drawer backs	$1/2$	$4^5/8$	9	
2	drawer fronts	$3/4$	$4^5/8$	10	$1/2$ x $1/2$ rabbet
2	drawer bottoms	$1/2$	$3^1/2$	9	
1	hook mounting plate	$3/4$	$3^1/2$	$18^3/4$	
2	hook brackets	$3/4$	$3^1/2$	6	
2	drawer knobs	$3/4$	$3/4$		
1	mirror	$1/8$	16	$26^1/4$	
3	coat hooks	Home Depot Online Shop #202045097			
8	storm window clips	Home Depot Online Shop #100555559			

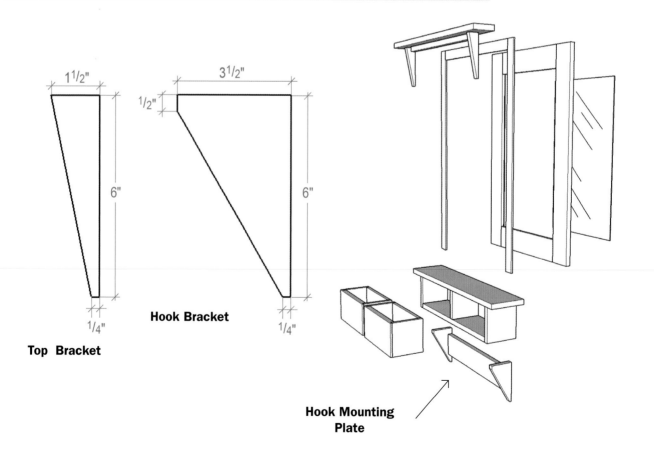

1½"

6"

¼"

Top Bracket

3½"

½"

6"

¼"

Hook Bracket

Hook Mounting Plate

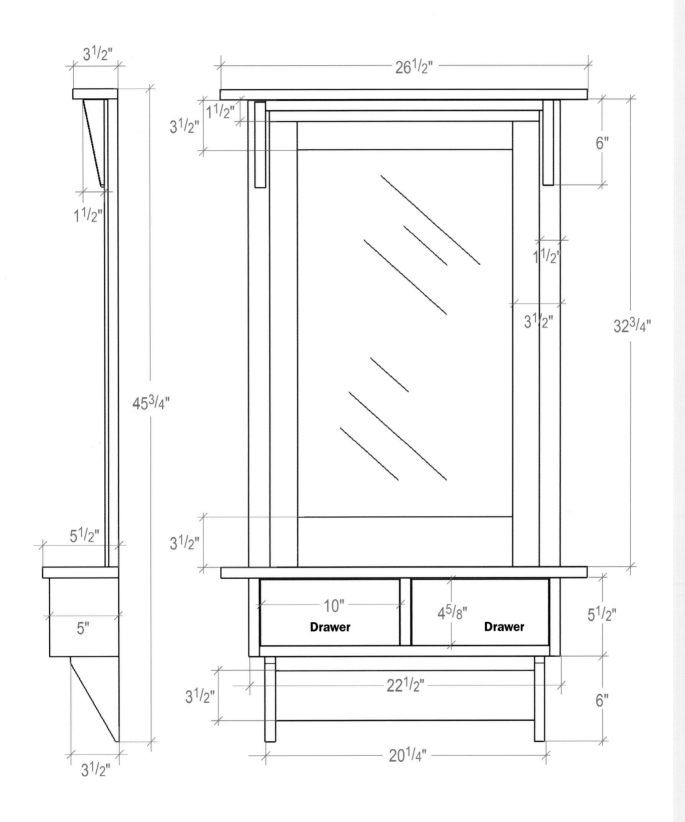

Shoji Screen

The shoji screen dates back as far as the 7th century, originating in China before appearing in Japan. The word "shoji" means "to obstruct" and that definition makes it a perfect room divider. Even though this project has an ancient past, it still has its place in the modern day.

A shoji screen is great for a large room you want to divide into individual spaces, or in a small room to hide unwanted items from view. It has rice paper on the upper section to allow light through and yet give privacy. The lower section has bamboo for an earthier, more rustic feel and appearance. The paper and bamboo are held in place on grids constructed with half-lap joints. The frame is simply some 1x2 and 1x4 poplar, making it extremely affordable and lightweight. The best part is that it has easily attached hinges so you can fold it up and store it away in a closet.

Start this project by gluing up the stiles for the screens. To achieve square stiles we're gluing four 1x2s (3/4" x 1 1/2") together. Start by cutting the twelve pieces to length, then glue and clamp two of the 1x2s together face-to-face **(Photo 1)**. Do the same to the others forming pairs of 1 1/2" x1 1/2" stiles.

While the stiles are drying, cut the three rails for each screen frame to length. The stiles are 1x4s and it's important that each of the rails is the exact same length. If not, keeping the frame square during assembly will be impossible. To help achieve this, use a stop block on your miter saw.

The distance from the edge of the blade to the edge of the stop block is set to the length of the rails. If the fence is not long enough on the miter saw for the length needed, clamp a scrap piece to the saw making an auxiliary fence **(Photo 2)**. Then clamp another scrap piece for the stop block. *NOTE – When cutting with a stop block it's important to let the blade come to a complete stop before lifting the blade up. Failure to do so could cause the blade to kick out the workpiece, causing damage to it or injury to you.*

The stiles are twice the thickness of the rails, so they won't be flush with the stile edges, but will instead be centered. This will give it a nice shadow line and reveal. Pocket screws are an option, but they leave visible holes on the back side. Since this screen will likely be viewed from both sides, we'll do the panel assembly on this project with dowel joinery.

Dowel joinery is done with a set of holes drilled into both

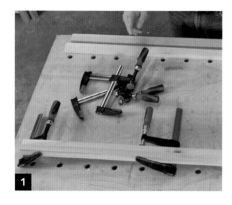

1

2

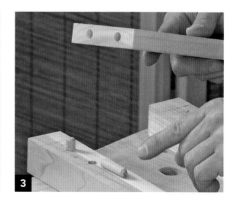

3

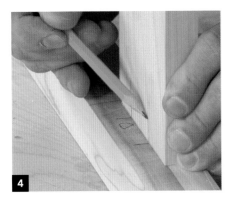

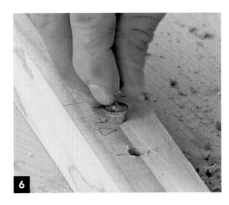

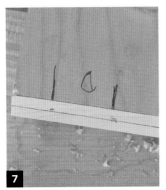

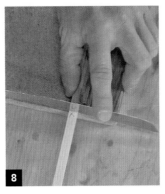

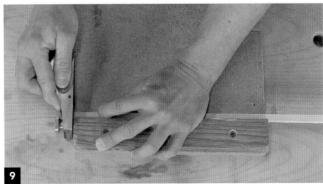

the stile and rail, with short dowel pins glued into the holes. The dowel pins have a slight chamfer on each end to make it easier to place in the holes, and also have small lengthwise grooves that allow good coverage of glue all around the pin for a strong hold **(Photo 3)**.

Use a doweling jig to properly position the holes so they line up correctly. This doweling jig has several sizes of holes for different sized dowel pins. It also has alignment marks so the holes will all line up when assembling the joints.

Center the rail on the stile in the correct position. Make two marks for where the dowel pins will go. The marks should be in line with each other across the rail onto the stile. It helps to also label the matching pieces with either a number or letter so as to not confuse them with other pieces **(Photo 4)**.

To drill the holes, use a drill bit that is the same size as the dowel pins (in this case 3/8"). A stop collar on the drill bit prevents drilling too deep into the workpieces **(Photo 5)**.

Repeat the same drilling procedure for the stiles.

If a doweling jig is not available, you can use small metal plugs with a sharp point on one end. Called "dowel centers" or "dowel points," when slipped into a hole these joinery aids correctly mark the location for matching holes. Find the center of both the stile and the rails and make pencil marks where the pins will go. Then drill the holes into the stiles and slip the dowel centers into the holes **(Photo 6)**.

Place the rail on top of the dowel centers, making sure the pencil marks line up. Then tap or apply pressure downward on the rail to make impressions from the pins into the end of rail **(Photo 7)**.

With the dimple marks made from the dowel centers as a guide, drill the 3/8" holes for the dowels in the rail.

Regardless which method you use to make the dowel holes, do a dry fit before adding any glue. Make sure the stiles and rails fit flush and they are square. If the dry fit is good then add glue, slip in the dowels and clamp the assembly up to dry.

While the frames are drying, make the grids for the screens. The grids are made out of 3/8" square stock that runs the length and width inside the frame. A nice and accurate way to measure the lengths and widths is to place one edge of the square stock inside the frame. Then at the opposite end simply mark where to cut the stock to fit inside. Remember to place an "X" on the waste side of the stock to avoid cutting it too short.

You can cut the square stock on a miter saw, but that seems like overkill for this narrow material. It's probably faster and easier to cut it with a bench hook and a handsaw **(Photo 8)**.

Make a bench hook out of some scrap. In my case, I used a 3/4" piece of plywood with cleats placed on opposite ends. One cleat goes against the edge of the bench, while the other cleat acts as a fence for cutting the stock.

After cutting, check the fit. If it's still a tad too tight you can use the bench hook as a shooting board with a plane. Place the stock against the cleat and use a block plane on its side, and shave off just a thin shaving with each pass. Then test the fit **(Photo 9)**.

The top and bottom sections of each screen frame use a pair of grids, with the paper or bamboo sandwiched between them. The top pair of grids use a total of 16 pieces (eight each). The bottom pair has eight (four each), making large

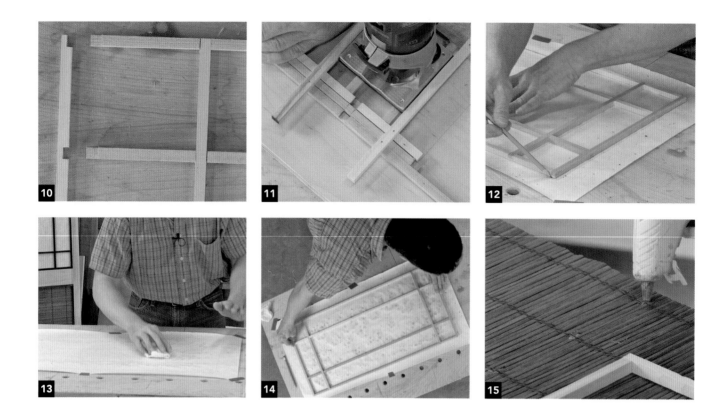

rectangles more so than actual grids. Keep track of the order and placement of each piece to avoid any inconsistency of the framework to ensure a good fit.

With all the square stock cut to length, begin construction of the grids using half-lap joinery **(Photo 10)**. Half lap joints are very strong because each piece interlocks to provide strength to prevent racking. Also the long grain on each piece gives a good glue surface for a strong bond.

To make the half-lap a strong joint, proper fit of the pieces is important. You could notch out the square stock with a handsaw and chisel, but there is a good chance of winding up with a sloppy fit of the two pieces. Instead make a simple jig for a router using some scrap pieces of leftover 3/8" square stock. The jig has two guides on each side of the router to control it. There are two more pieces under the router to act as a track and raise it up off the plywood base. There are also two fences to support the workpiece that goes in between it. The two fences not only help house the workpiece, but they also help eliminate tear-out as the router bit passes through.

Chuck a 3/8" bit into the router and set the depth to 3/16", half the thickness of the material.

Keep in mind, the size of your jig varies depending on size of your router. And it's a good idea to do a few test cuts on some scrap pieces before cutting the actual workpieces **(Photo 11)**.

With all the half-lap joints cut, you can begin the glue up. You could use spring clamps at each joint to apply pressure while drying, but that would require a lot of clamps. A simpler way is to wrap each joint with masking tape. The joint itself is already a good fit, but the pressure from the tape just aids in a good bond for the glue.

When the grids are dry do a test fit in the frame. It's possible the grids came out of square while the glue was drying, so you may need to do some minor shaving with a block plane to get a snug fit.

The grids aren't held in place with glue. Reason being, there will be paper between each grid. If the paper ever rips or gets a hole in it, it would be really hard to remove the grid to replace the paper. So drill tiny pilot holes around the outside pieces of the grid for nails to go in. Drill the holes on a slight angle so when the nails are hammered in, the swinging of the hammer minimizes the risk of hitting the inner grid pieces.

With the grids fit to the frame and drilled for nails, but not installed, the next step is to apply the paper. *NOTE – If you plan to paint, stain or finish the grid, do that before applying paper.* Lay the paper out and place the grid on top of the paper. Then trace around the outside edge of the grid **(Photo 12)**.

Brush a small amount of glue only on the outer edge of the grid frame. This is because if the paper ever tears it will be easier to remove in the future. Lightly dampen the paper with some water. The water helps to relax the paper. When the paper later dries, it will shrink just a little making for a nice, taut appearance **(Photo 13)**.

Place the grid onto the paper **(Photo 14)**. The glue should dry pretty quickly, but to help get a good even bond, place a sheet of plywood on top to apply even pressure across the entire grid. Once the glue has dried, use a razor blade or knife to trim off the excess paper around the edges. *NOTE –*

Paper is applied only to one of the top grids.

The bottom grid rectangles have bamboo blinds instead of paper. Open the blind up and remove any metal or unwanted items attached to the blind. *NOTE – One blind is probably big enough to make multiple screens.*

To fit the screen frame you'll need to cut the blinds to the correct length and width. To shorten the blinds to length, place the grid atop the blind and mark cut lines on the blinds with a pencil. Cutting the blind to length means cutting through the stitching, which would unravel the individual pieces of the blind. To prevent this, use a small dab of hot glue across both of the stitchings **(Photo 15)**. With a razor blade, cut on the waste side of the glue dab **(Photo 16)**.

To save the rest of the blind for future use, apply more glue to the stitching to prevent unraveling, and store it away.

To cut the blinds to width, first roll them up as tight as possible. Wrap both ends of the blind with tape to keep the roll in place. Wrap tape around the area where the cut lines are to avoid splintering. The blind is most easily cut with a fine toothed hand saw **(Photo 17)**.

Once the blind is cut to width and height of the screen frame, apply glue around the edge of a lower grid rectangle and place the unrolled blind on it. Use spring clamps at the corners and some tape on the sides to hold the blind in place until the glue dries **(Photo 18)**.

When the grids are dry, begin final assembly by placing the grid without any paper on it into the frame. With the grid sitting flush against the frame, tap a nail part way into the grid. Set a combination square for the distance that the grid needs to set back on the stiles, and then tap the nail all the

way through the grid and into the frame **(Photo 19)**. When the "empty" grid frames are in place, attach the papered and bamboo panels atop them, sandwiching the paper and bamboo between them, and nail in place the same way.

With both upper and lower grid panels in place, one of the shoji screens is done. You can make several of these in the same manner and add as many of them as desired. But connecting them together requires a pair of butt hinges.

It doesn't really matter where you place the hinges on the frame. Since these hinges act mostly as a means of joining the shoji screens together, a simple face mounting is all that is required. However, the direction the hinges face is important. Make sure the barrel of the hinges face outward from the frame to allow the hinges to swing fully open and closed **(Photo 20)**.

It's not a bad idea before placing the screws and attaching the hinges to first add a finish to the shoji screens. I used an oil-based exterior polyurethane finish because this particular poly has a slight amber hue to it. However, because this project is never used outdoors, a more practical finish is a water-based poly which will dry very fast allowing multiple coats in a single day. Use a foam brush to apply the poly for a smooth finish and the brush can just be tossed out when done. Remember to sand between each coat of poly with #220-grit paper to build up a smooth and durable finish.

Having a shoji screen gives you a clear understand why this piece has been around for centuries. Once you have one you'll agree it is a piece of future that will stay in your household for a long, long time.

Parts list in inches

QTY.	PART	THICKNESS	WIDTH	LENGTH	NOTES
2	posts	$1\frac{1}{2}$	$1\frac{1}{2}$	72	
3	rails	$\frac{3}{4}$	$3\frac{1}{2}$	15	half-lap joinery
8	vertical strips (top)	$\frac{3}{8}$	$\frac{3}{8}$	32	half-lap joinery
8	horizontal strips (top)	$\frac{3}{8}$	$\frac{3}{8}$	15	half-lap joinery
4	vertical strips (bottom)	$\frac{3}{8}$	$\frac{3}{8}$	$25\frac{1}{4}$	half-lap joinery
4	drawer front	$\frac{3}{8}$	$\frac{3}{8}$	15	half-lap joinery
shoji paper		purchase at: http://www.eshoji.com/c/shoji-paper.html			
bamboo blends		Home Depot Online Shop #204597442 or at store #1000024911			

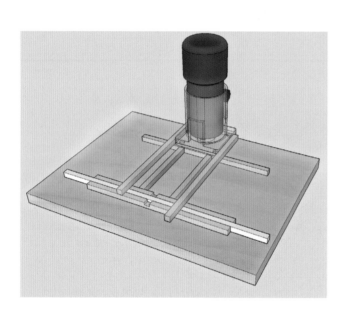

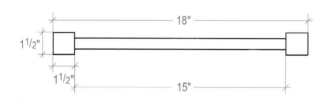

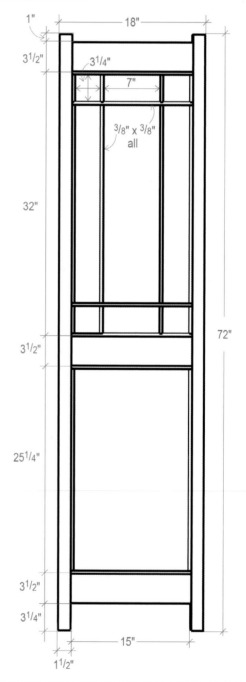

Backyard Bar

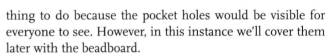

For many of us, summertime conjures up images of backyards, parties and BBQ's. Of course, at any BBQ, cold drinks are required. What's better than somewhere to not only store the cold drinks, but a place to serve them as well?

This backyard bar is perfect for doing just that. It is 42" tall, which is ideal for any standard-height barstool. It has a footrest for guests to comfortably rest their feet. On the other side, the host has a countertop at a convenient 30" height and a lower shelf for storage. The best part is that an integrated lid in the countertop lifts to reveal a hidden cooler to store ice for cold beverages. The cooler has a drain plug to let out water from melted ice when the party's over. The bar is finished off with some handsome beadboard and easy stick-down tiles for a decorative and protective bar and countertop.

From the plans, cut the 1x4s to length on the miter saw for the rails and stiles (or legs) for the sides. You'll use pocket screws to join these pieces. Drill pocket holes on the rails to attach to the stiles, keeping the pocket holes facing what will be the outside. Normally, this would be an odd thing to do because the pocket holes would be visible for everyone to see. However, in this instance we'll cover them later with the beadboard.

Use glue and pocket screws to attach the rails to the stiles on both sides. Each side should be a mirror image to the other **(Photo 1)**.

Cut the pieces to length for the rails that go on the front and back of the bar. All of these pieces are cut from 1x4 stock except the lower front rail. This rail is cut from 1x8 to allow sufficient height for the footrest brackets to be screwed into place in a later step. Just as before, use pocket screws to attach the rails to the sides. There's also two smaller blocks (5½" x 6½") that are in place to support the upper shelf. These are held in place with pocket screws into the rail and back support, again using pocket screws from the outside.

Also, drill some pocket holes in the upper edge of the inner left sides of the two top rails. We'll use those holes later when attaching the countertop. No need for them on

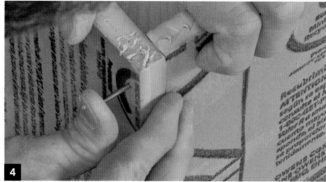

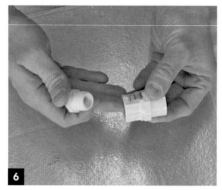

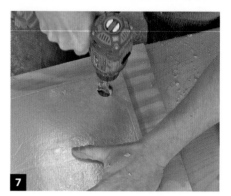

the right side, as that's where the hinged lift-up lid to the cooler will go **(Photo 2)**.

With the overall frame structure for the bar complete, turn your attention to the countertop. The countertop is made from ³/₄" particleboard which is smooth and flat – great for the peel-and-stick adhesive tiles to go on later **(Photo 3)**.

The lower shelf could just as easily have the particleboard and tiles, but it won't really be seen. So there is no reason to waste tiles on it since it will be out of view from most people. An easy alternative is some BC grade plywood and it will adequately do the job.

When cutting any kind of plywood make sure to have a few sacrificial boards underneath to prevent cutting into the benchtop or sawhorses. Make sure the cut is perpendicular to the sacrificial boards to prevent the plywood from falling inward on itself and pinching the saw blade.

To achieve a straight cut, use a circular saw cutting jig for dead-on accuracy.

Once cut, don't attach the countertop and lower shelf pieces yet. Instead, make the cooler first so you have enough room to set it in place.

The cooler is made up of foamboard insulation. From the cut list, lay out the measurements and use a razor knife to cut the individual pieces that will make up the cooler. It's not a bad idea to use a scrap piece of wood underneath to protect the benchtop work surface.

Once the pieces are cut, temporarily hold them together with some ring shank nails. The nails will easily push through the foamboard, and the tiny rings around the nails help hold the pieces in place without backing out **(Photo 4)**.

The bottom piece sits inside the cooler sides. Place the cooler on top of the foamboard with one corner of the foamboard tight against one inside corner of the cooler. With a pencil, trace the opposite corner edges and then cut the piece of foamboard **(Photo 5)**. Don't worry too much if the pieces have slight gaps in them. That will be taken care of soon.

Before assembling the cooler, first install a drain plug into the bottom piece of foamboard. The drain plug consists of two PVC plumbing parts with a male plug that screws into a female adapter **(Photo 6)**. Measure the size of the female adapter and drill a hole into one corner of the bottom with the appropriate size drill bit **(Photo 7)**. I placed my drain in the front left corner of the bottom. You may prefer a different location.

Place the bottom into the cooler. It should fit slightly snug. The bottom should have a slope to it so the water will flow toward the drain plug. At the opposite corner from the plug, place a small scrap of foamboard underneath to slightly raise up the corner **(Photo 8)**. And then again, push ring shank

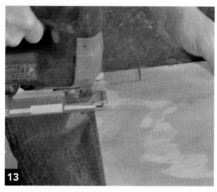

nails through the sides to hold the bottom in place.

When putting the nails in the bottom, use a combination square and measure the portion of the bottom that is sloped. Then transfer that measurement to the outside edge to place the nails correctly on the first try. Unwanted holes in the cooler are just potential places for leaks.

After the nails are in, wrap duct tape around the outside corners. The tape is not what will seal cooler, but it does add strength to the construction **(Photo 9)**.

Seal all the inside corners with 100% silicone caulk, which will any gaps from uneven cuts **(Photo 10)**. Silicone dries by using moisture, but when it cures it's 100% waterproof. Make sure that the drain plug is sealed well.

The cooler rests inside the bar on a couple more 1x4s. Make sure to drill pilot holes in the 1x4s so they don't split, then screw them to the frame **(Photo 11)**. *NOTE – Make sure that the placement of the 1x4s does not interfere with the drain plug.*

Place the cooler in position and use a couple of screws to attach it to the frame **(Photo 12)**.

The countertop is attached from underneath. The rails have already been drilled for pocket holes. Use some clamps to hold the top down and square it up with the frame. Drive pocket screws up through the rail and into the underside of countertop.

Now, cut the cooler lid to size and set it aside for installation a bit later.

Cut the lower shelf to size. The front legs interfere with setting it in place, so notch the corners with a jigsaw so it will fit around the legs **(Photo 13)**.

Place the lower shelf into position. It could be pocket-screwed in place, but it's simpler to glue and nail it in place **(Photo 14)**.

The outside of the bar is wrapped in beadboard picked up at the big box store. It is 1/4" thick and has tongue-and-groove joints on the sides – tongue on one side, groove on the other. Whenever laying out beadboard, whether for wall covering in a house or for this project, follow this rule for a nice look. Find the center of the project, and glue and nail the first piece in place there. Then work from the center to the outside edges. This ensures that each end piece is of equal size. This method eliminates an odd size piece at the end causing an unbalanced look.

The beadboard is solid wood, and wood wants to expand and contract. For that reason, use just a dab of glue in the center of each board. That way the outer edges still have room to move.

Working from the middle to the ends will leave the last boards on the front too wide, so rip them down to fit. However, make sure the last front end pieces are 1/4" longer

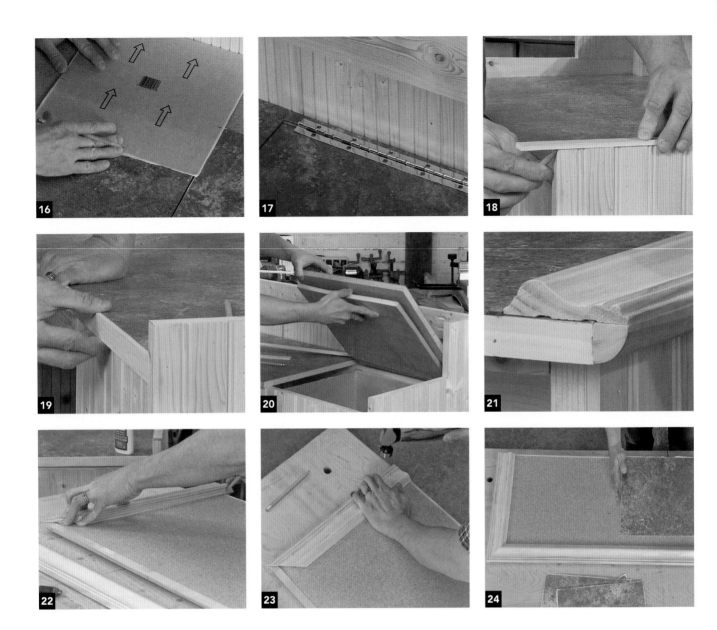

than the frame. As the side beadboard is placed on, this forms a nice corner without any gaps for a nice, flush fit **(Photo 15)**.

Self-adhesive tiles are placed on the countertop and cooler lid (the lid is still unattached at this point). Although the tiles have a sticky adhesive, it may not be enough in extreme temperature changes. So as a suggestion, use extra spray adhesive before setting the tiles.

Setting the full tiles is a no brainer, but precisely fitting smaller pieces can be tricky.

To measure for the smaller pieces, turn the tiles upside down. Then, keeping one edge to the back, mark with a pencil where the full tile's edge is. Use a straightedge and score the tile with a knife, then the tile should easily snap. Then stick it in place **(Photo 16)**.

With all the tiles in place, mount the cooler lid's hinge. We've already set tiles on the lid and the mounting rail at the back separately, so there is no need to cut around the hinge. Make sure there are even gaps going all the way around the lid, then drill mounting holes with a self-centering drill bit and drive in the screws **(Photo 17)**.

The edges of the frame and beadboard have a rough, unfinished look to them. We'll use some doorstop from the trim selection at the big box store to give it a clean, finished look. Lay a trim piece on top and mark it with a pencil. Cut it on the miter saw, then glue and nail it in place **(Photo 18)**.

Cut some of the same doorstop trim for the front edge of the countertop and cooler lid. It covers up the edge of the particleboard and gives it a nice, finished look **(Photo 19)**.

To make sure drinks stay extra cold, screw a piece of insulation foamboard to the underside of the lid **(Photo 20)**.

Next, we'll create the bar top. It's made from particleboard with a homemade bar rail around it.

Actual bar rail can be expensive and you'd normally have to go to a custom mill shop to have one created. But this clever one is made up of chair-rail molding and some 3/4" quarter-round trim **(Photo 21)**.

Use the door trim to cover up the particleboard edge.

The trim is wider than the particleboard so after it is glued and nailed on, use a block plane and plane it flush. Next is the quarter-round on each side and the front edge. Begin on one side with a straight crosscut at the back edge. At the front edge, mark with a pencil and cut it at 45° on the miter saw. Drill, nail and glue the quarter-round to the side. Then continue measuring, cutting and attaching the trim around the front and the other side **(Photo 22)**.

With the quarter round done, the chair rail is next. Cut a 45° angle on the miter saw first, then line up the angled end at the front corner, leaving it long at the back. Mark the back end of the chair rail and cut it off so it's flush with the countertop's rear edge **(Photo 23)**. Glue and nail the chair rail on and then repeat the process for the other pieces.

When attaching the peel-and-stick tiles to the bar top, it's tempting to start laying the tiles at one end and work to the other side. But if you do the last tile won't be a full piece. So a better way is to start at the middle and work to each edge, as we did with the beadboard **(Photo 24)**.

Cut and fit the smaller tile pieces in the same manner as on the countertop. This completes the bar top, but don't attach it yet.

Turn the bar on its side and attach baseboard molding around the bottom. Measure and cut the baseboard in the same manner as the other trim – cut at 45° on the miter saw, then glue and nail into place. Just as before, start at one side and work around the front to the opposite side **(Photo 25)**.

The foot rail goes on next, and since we're using a length of standard staircase handrail for this, we'll also use handrail brackets here. Since they're designed to mount on wall studs, these brackets come with long screws **(Photo 26)**.

The frame of the bar is made out of ³/₄"-thick wood. And because a lot of pressure is applied when resting feet on the foot rail, add an extra support block on the inside of the bar so the bracket screws have plenty of meat to bite into. This is just a square of ³/₄" plywood screwed to the inside of the lower front rail **(Photo 27)**.

Drill pilot holes and mount the brackets to the bar front, making sure the screws go into the support block on the inside. Then, drill pilot holes on the underside of the rail and screw the rail in place atop the brackets.

Before attaching the bar top, prepare the frame by adding a brace on the frame. This will give the bar top more stability, as well as provide a way to attach the top. Use pocket screws to attach a 1x4 going across the frame **(Photo 28)**.

Now, apply glue to the brace and drive screws up through the brace into the underside of the bar top. When placing the bar top to the frame, keep in mind the overhang at the front. If it's too much where the guest sits, the bar could tip if they lean on it too hard. However, too much overhang on the side of where the bartender is will interfere with fully opening the ice chest lid. I positioned my with a 2" overhang on the inside, leaving a 7³/₄" overhang to the front **(Photo 29)**.

For the finish, it depends on where you plan to use your bar. The wood used on this project is generally intended for interior use, so if you use it outside a good exterior paint, stain or finish is required. And I'd suggest that when not in use to drape it with a protective covering to help shield it against the elements.

Whether in the backyard, or in a man cave, this bar will be a nice place for friends to gather while sipping on a refreshing cool beverage.

Parts list in inches

QTY.	PART	THICKNESS	WIDTH	LENGTH
4	horizontal supports	$3/4$	$3^1/2$	$43^1/2$
3	horizontal supports	$3/4$	$3^1/2$	38
1	horizontal supports	$3/4$	$7^1/4$	38
6	horizontal supports	$3/4$	$3^1/2$	$15^3/4$
2	vertical supports	$3/4$	$3^1/2$	34
2	vertical supports	$3/4$	$3^1/2$	$40^1/2$
2	upper shelf supports	$3/4$	$5^1/2$	$6^1/2$
2	lower shelf & top	$3/4$	$18^1/2$	26
1	ice bin lid*	$3/4$	$17^1/2$	$18^1/2$
2	ice bin supports	$3/4$	$3^1/2$	$18^1/2$
2	ice bin sides (insul.)	$5/8$	$13^1/2$	$16^1/4$
2	ice bin sides (insul.)	$5/8$	$13^1/2$	16

QTY.	PART	THICKNESS	WIDTH	LENGTH
1	ice bin bottom (insul.)	$5/8$	16	15
1	bar top	$3/4$	$15^1/4$	48
solid edging		$1/4$	$1^1/16$	140

32 sq. ft. of tongue-in-groove paneling

8 lineal feet of base board

8 lineal feet of chair rail

8 lineal feet of $3/4$" quarter round

4 lineal feet of hand rail

2 hand rail supports

16 sq. ft. of adhesive tile

*cut lid to create $3/4$" top edge at rear

FRAMING VIEWS

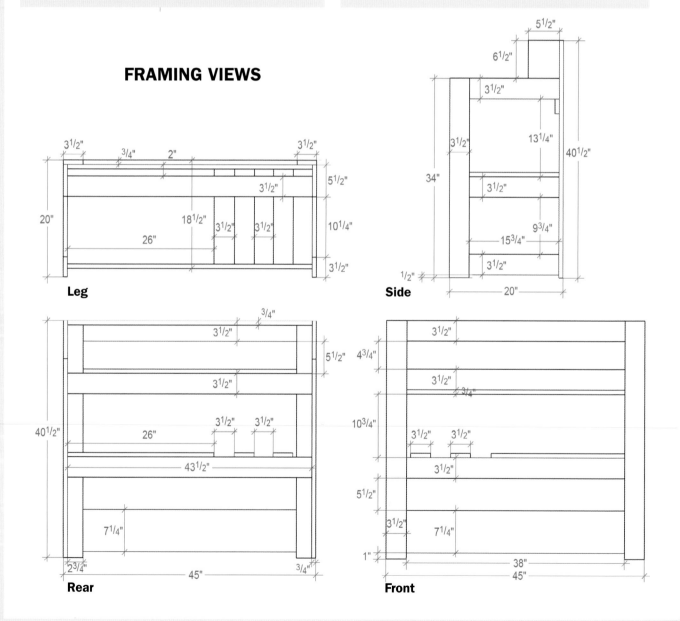

Leg

Side

Rear

Front

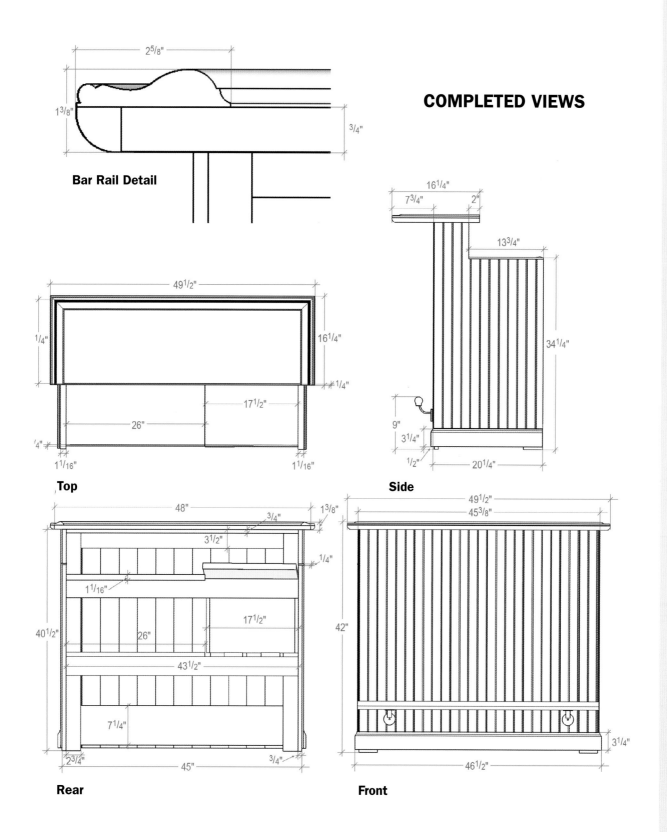

Bar Rail Detail

COMPLETED VIEWS

Top

Side

Rear

Front

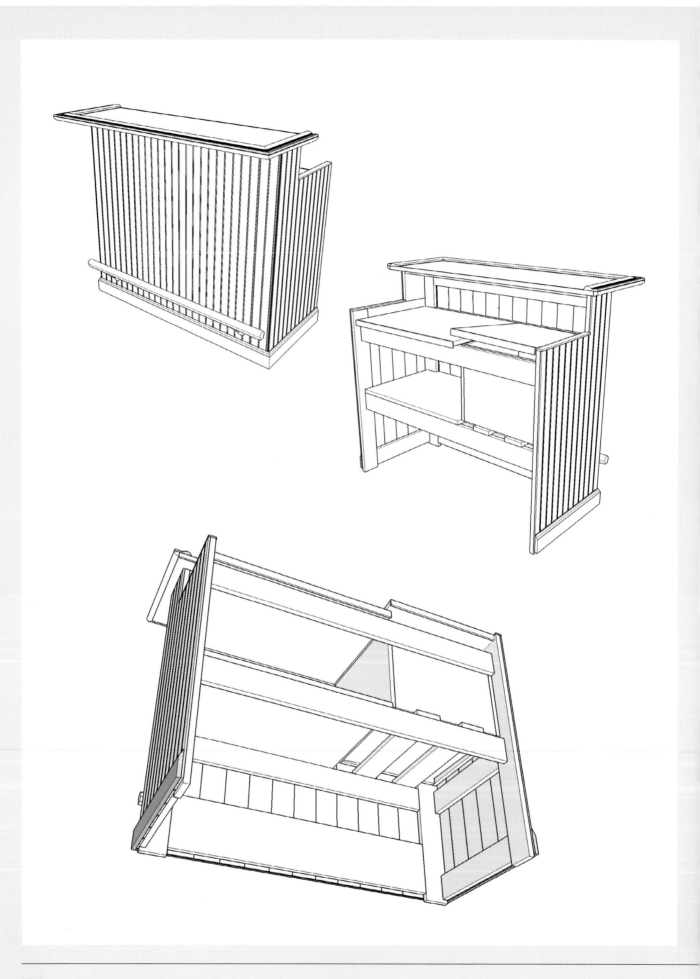

Potting Bench

This outdoor potting bench was designed for the person with a green thumb. It has a large working surface, a tray for dirt or potting soil, a tool tray to hold a kneepad and small trowel and plenty of shelves to accommodate a variety of different-sized flowerpots. But this bench doesn't have to be limited to the gardener in your life. It could just as easily be a hobbyist's workbench.

This is a larger project and is constructed with numerous components of varying sizes. When selecting the lumber, take time to find boards that are straight and flat. Remove any staples or nails on the boards that might hold stickers; those can cause damage to your blade when making the various cuts.

You'll also need a few other items that are unique to this project besides the lumber. Because this bench is intended for outdoor use, exterior-grade screws and water-resistant or waterproof glue are also required.

Begin your build with the aprons that make up the frame for the benchtop. Using the plans and measurements, crosscut the front, back and side aprons on the miter saw, then drill clearance holes through the ends of the side aprons. (Clearance holes should be slightly larger than the diameter of the screw; they prevent the board from splitting when a screw goes through.) Glue and screw the sides to the front and back aprons **(Photo 1)**.

Using the measurements from the cut list and the same construction procedure, repeat the process for the rails that make up the lower shelf assembly.

The lower shelf unit has a series of 12 slats that are attached widthwise. When making multiple pieces of the same length, attach a stop block to the saw to make accurate repetitive cuts **(Photo 2)**. *NOTE – When using a stop block, make sure the blade comes to a complete stop before lifting the blade or removing the workpiece. Failure to do so could result in*

workpiece damage or personal injury.

Before attaching the slats, make sure the lower rail assembly is square. Use a tape measure and check the dimensions diagonally from opposite corners. If one measurement is longer than the other, compress the longer side and recheck until measurements are the same.

As mentioned before, these slats will run the width (front to back) of the lower section. You could screw the slats in place, but screws are expensive so nails and glue are a better alternative. The slats should have a 3/8" space between each of them that allows airflow and water to run off the lower section. *TIP – Instead of measuring the 3/8" spacing, use a shim as a spacer* **(Photo 3)**.

When all the slats are glued and nailed in place, set the

completed assembly aside. Now, check the upper apron assembly for square in the same manner that was done with the lower rail assembly. Unlike the lower rail assembly where the slats run the width, the benchtop boards run the length of the apron assembly, spanning the middle of the framework. To prevent the boards bowing, add a middle 2x4 support. Place the assembly upside down on the workbench to keep the support flush with the top edge of the aprons. Drill clearance holes in the aprons, then glue and screw the support across the middle of the frame **(Photo 4)**.

Turn the frame right-side up, and with the three benchtop pieces already cut to length on the miter saw, position the rear board atop the frame. This 1x8 board should be flush with the back edge of the frame, and overhang 1" on each side **(Photo 5)**.

Next, place the 1x6 for the middle, and another 1x8 for the front. Just like the rear board, these also overhang at the sides, and the front board overhangs the front edge. Make sure to keep a slight gap between boards for water and

loose soil to fall through. Screw the boards to the aprons and to the middle support. *NOTE – Do not use glue on these boards. The bench is intended for outdoor use and the boards may warp and crack over time due to exposure to the elements. By not applying any glue, you can easily replace the boards at a later date if damage should occur.*

Set the benchtop assembly aside and move on to making the upper hutch shelf assembly. Cut the sides, top and bottom shelves and cleats to length on the miter saw. Begin by gluing and nailing the rear cleats to the underside of the top shelf and the upper side of the bottom shelf. We'll use these cleats to attach the hutch assembly to the rear legs later. Glue and screw the side pieces to the top and bottom shelves **(Photo 6)**.

Now, connect a middle divider to the top and bottom shelf. However, with the added cleats, the middle divider is too wide and not flush with the front of the shelves, so notch the back corners of the divider to fit around the cleats. Place the divider in its proper position and mark with a pencil where the divider contacts the cleat **(Photo 7)**. Then cut out these areas with a jigsaw and test the fit).

Once you've achieved a nice fit, screw and glue the middle divider and shelf in place **(Photo 8)**.

With the hutch assembly complete, crosscut the required pieces for the dirt tray to length on miter saw. Place the two shorter pieces on your workbench and measure for the placement of handles. Make the handle by drilling a series of $3/4$" holes through it. After the holes are drilled, use a chisel to trim off the high points and form the handle **(Photo 9)**.

Finish the handle by smoothing it with a file or sandpaper. Repeat the process for the other side. Glue and nail the

handle pieces to the remaining longer pieces to form the outer framework of the tray.

A bottom goes inside the tray, but a 1x10 is slightly too wide to fit. Place the tray on top of 1x10, fitting one corner of the 1x10 tightly into a corner of the tray. With a pencil, trace the opposite edges. Then crosscut and rip the 1x10 to size and test the fit. Once a nice snug fit is achieved, glue and nail the bottom into the tray.

The tray slides into a shelf on one side of the bench. The tray shelf consists of a bottom, a back and one side that are glued and screwed together. There is only one side to this shelf; the other side is the end of the bench **(Photo 10)**.

We'll attach the tray shelf to the bench later with metal angle brackets during final assembly.

This bench also has a tool tray for storing a knee pad or towel. Four simple pieces form this tool tray with tapered 1x6s for the sides. On one of the pieces, measure over 4" at the top and 3/8" at bottom. Connect the two points with a straightedge and then cut with a jigsaw **(Photo 11)**. After cutting, smooth out the rough edges with a block plane. Repeat for the other side. Glue and nail the front on and then the back **(Photo 12)**.

Once together there should be a small gap at the bottom of the tray so it doesn't hold water when it rains, or stray potting soil brushed off the benchtop.

The final section to tackle before assembly is the hutch supports. These two supports are made from a 2x4 with a decorative pattern cut into the outer ends. This pattern is optional, but easy to create by tracing the curves off various sized cans. Or, you could draw them free-hand to whatever shape you desire **(Photo 13)**.

Cut out the shape on the supports with a jigsaw, then sand smooth.

Final assembly is pretty straightforward, as the front and rear legs attach everything together to form the potting bench. I recommend not using glue during assembly so the whole potting bench can be disassembled and stored away in the garage or shed.

The back legs are much longer than the front and it's important that the legs are attached to the lower shelf and benchtop assembly at the same height to prevent rocking or unevenness. Gang the legs together and using measurements from the cut list, pencil in lines designating where the various pieces are fastened.

Attach the benchtop assembly to the rear legs first.

Lay the back legs flat on the floor and place the benchtop assembly on the designated line. Drill a series of pilot holes through the apron, but only place one screw on each side for now **(Photo 14)**.

Measure the distance between the two legs with a tape measure. Make sure the distance between them is the same at the top and bottom to ensure the legs are straight and square. That one screw allows the legs to pivot if an adjustment is needed to achieve an equal measurement **(Photo 15)**. When square, drive in the remaining screws to lock in the positions of the legs and fasten the benchtop assembly in place.

As with the benchtop, place the lower shelf assembly in its designated place. Then drill clearance holes through the rails and screw the assembly to the rear legs **(Photo 16)**.

Place the front legs on and drill pilot holes, then screw the front legs to the benchtop apron and the lower shelf rail **(Photo 17)**.

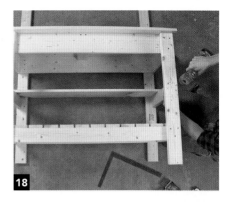

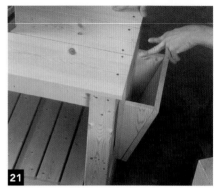

Between the benchtop and lower shelf is a shallow middle shelf. The middle shelf is a 1x8 with 2x4 supports screwed to the ends. This assembly is slid into the potting bench and mounted between the front and rear legs. To attach it firmly in place, drill pilot holes through the front and rear legs, and then secure the shelf with 2½" screws driven into the ends of the supports **(Photo 18)**.

Stand the potting bench up and place the hutch shelf on the benchtop. Drill the sides of the hutch assembly and attach the top supports to the outside edge of the assembly with screws. Place the top boards across the supports so the rear board overhangs the supports by 1½" at the back. This will allow you to carefully lift the hutch assembly and rest it atop the rear legs. (The hutch assembly is heavy, so you may want to ask a friend for assistance lifting it.) Once in place, drill pilot holes and screw the top boards to the supports **(Photo 19)**.

With a couple of clearance holes through the cleats on the shelves, screw the hutch to the rear legs **(Photo 20)**.

The tool tray easily mounts to the side legs with just two screws **(Photo 21)**.

At the opposite side of bench, mount the brackets to the legs. Then place the tray shelf on the brackets and screw through the underside of the brackets into the tray shelf **(Photo 22)**.

Test fit the dirt tray on the tray shelf. Minor adjustments to the shelf may be necessary or you may need to plane the tray to make it fit.

At this point the potting bench construction is done. Give everything a good sanding before applying any finish.

You can use any good exterior paint or deck stain as a finish, but another old method to protect the wood is a combination of boiled linseed oil and turpentine with a ratio of 50/50. The linseed oil gives good exterior protection and the turpentine thins out the linseed oil, allowing the mixture to soak deeper into the wood. This will help protect the bench from water damage.

Remember to seal the bottom of the legs with a few coats of exterior glue; otherwise the end grain can wick water deep into the wood.

Your potting bench will look great in the backyard with flowers on it. Besides being useful for the gardener, it also makes a great project to "grow" your woodworking skills.

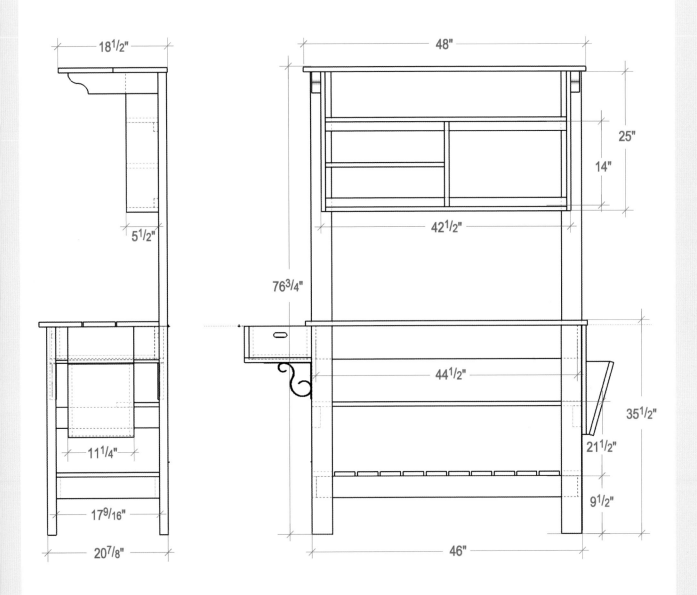

Parts list in inches

QTY.	PART	THICKNESS	WIDTH	LENGTH
2	front legs	$1^1/_2$	$3^1/_2$	$34^1/_4$
2	back legs	$1^1/_2$	$3^1/_2$	76
2	top supports	$1^1/_2$	$3^1/_2$	$15^1/_4$
2	side braces	$1^1/_2$	$3^1/_2$	$17^9/_{16}$
2	bench top	$3/_4$	$7^1/_4$	48
1	bench top	$3/_4$	$5^1/_2$	48
2	F & B aprons	$3/_4$	$5^1/_2$	$44^1/_2$
2	side aprons	$3/_4$	$5^1/_2$	$17^9/_{16}$
2	F & B bottom shelf	$3/_4$	$3^1/_2$	$44^1/_2$
2	shelf sides	$3/_4$	$3^1/_2$	$17^9/_{16}$
12	lower slats	$3/_4$	$3^1/_2$	$17^9/_{16}$
1	middle shelf	$3/_4$	$7^1/_4$	46
2	hutch top(s)	$3/_4$	$9^1/_4$	48
2	hutch sides	$3/_4$	$5^1/_2$	23
2	hutch shelves	$3/_4$	$5^1/_2$	41
1	hutch shelf	$3/_4$	$5^1/_2$	$20^1/_8$
1	hutch divider	$3/_4$	$5^1/_2$	14
2	hutch cleats	$3/_4$	$1^1/_2$	41
2	tool tray sides	$3/_4$	4	12
1	tool tray front	$3/_4$	$11^1/_4$	$12^1/_2$
1	tool tray back	$3/_4$	$11^1/_4$	18
1	tray shelf bottom	$3/_4$	$11^1/_4$	$19^1/_4$
1	tray shelf side	$3/_4$	$5^1/_4$	$19^1/_4$
1	tray shelf back	$3/_4$	$5^1/_4$	$10^1/_2$
2	tray sides	$3/_4$	$5^1/_2$	$16^3/_4$
2	tray ends	$3/_4$	$5^1/_2$	$10^1/_2$
1	tray bottom	$3/_4$	9	$16^3/_4$

1 square = 1 inch

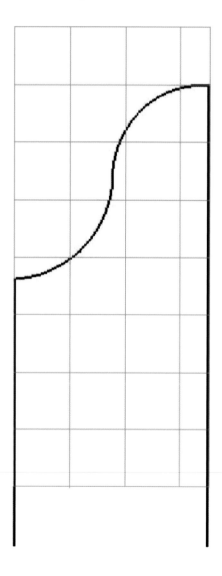

Distributed in Canada by Fraser Direct
100 Armstrong Avenue
Georgetown, Ontario L7G 5S4
Canada

Distributed in the U.K. and Europe by
F+W Media International, LTD
Pynes Hill Court
Pynes Hill
Rydon Lane
Exeter
EX2 5SP
Tel: +44 1392 797680

a content + ecommerce company

Visit our website at popularwoodworking.com or our consumer website at shopwoodworking.com for more woodworking information.

Other fine Popular Woodworking Books are available from your local bookstore or direct from the publisher.

ISBN-13: 978-1-4403-5123-5

22 21 20 19 18   5 4 3 2 1

EDITORS:
Scott Francis, A.J. Hamler and David Thiel
DESIGNERS:
Danielle Lowery and Laura Spencer
PRODUCTION COORDINATOR:
Debbie Thomas

METRIC CONVERSION CHART

to convert	to	multiply by
Inches	Centimeters	2.54
Centimeters	Inches	0.4
Feet	Centimeters	30.5
Centimeters	Feet	0.03
Yards	Meters	0.9
Meters	Yards	1.1

To view the online *I Can Do That Manual* on using the tools and basic information on woodworking used in these projects, visit the address below.

http://bit.ly/ICDT_Manual

Ideas • Instruction • Inspiration

Get downloadable woodworking instructions when you sign up
for our free newsletter at **popularwoodworking.com**.

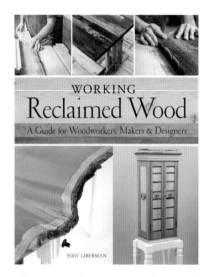

Visit **popularwoodworking.com** to subscribe (look for the red "Subscribe" button on the navigation bar).

These and other great Popular Woodworking products are available at your local bookstore, woodworking store or online supplier. Visit our website at **shopwoodworking.com**.

Popular Woodworking Videos

Subscribe and get immediate access to the web's best woodworking subscription site. You'll find more than 400 hours of woodworking video tutorials and full-length video workshops from world-class instructors on workshops, projects, SketchUp, tools, techniques and more!

videos.popularwoodworking.com

Visit our Website

Fiid helpful and inspiring articles, videos, blogs, projects and plans at **popularwoodworking.com**.

 For behind the scenes information, become a fan at **Facebook.com/popularwoodworking**.

 For more tips, clips and articles, follow us at **twitter.com/pweditors**.

 For visual inspiration, follow us at **pinterest.com/popwoodworking**.

 For free videos visit **youtube.com/popularwoodworking**.

 Follow us on Instagram **@popularwoodworking**.